ENGLISH DRAMATISTS

VANBRUGH
&
FARQUHAR

John Bull

Professor of Film and Drama, University of Reading

First published 1998 by
MACMILLAN PRESS LTD
Houndmills, Basingstoke, Hampshire RG21 6XS
and London
Companies and representatives
throughout the world

ISBN 0–333–46232–7 hardcover
ISBN 0–333–46233–5 paperback

A catalogue record for this book is available
from the British Library.

This book is printed on paper suitable for recycling and made
from fully managed and sustained forest sources.

10	9	8	7	6	5	4	3	2	1
07	06	05	04	03	02	01	00	99	98

Printed in Malaysia

Published in the United States of America 1998 by
ST. MARTIN'S PRESS, INC.,
Scholarly and Reference Division
175 Fifth Avenue, New York, N.Y. 10010

ISBN 0–312–21268–2

For Carole and Lydia

Contents

Editor's Preface

Each generation needs to be introduced to the culture and great works of the past and to reinterpret them in its own ways. This series re-examines the important English dramatists of earlier centuries in the light of new information, new interests and new attitudes. The books are written for students, theatre-goers and general readers who want an up-to-date view of the plays and dramatists, with emphasis on drama as theatre and on stage, social and political history. Attention is given to what is known about performance, acting styles, changing interpretations, the stages and theatres of the time and theatre economics. The books will be relevant to those interested in or studying literature, theatre and cultural history.

BRUCE KING

Acknowledgements

This book must serve as an extremely belated acknowledgement of the debt of gratitude owed by me to Howard Erskine-Hill for first interesting and then involving me in the period. I am grateful to the British Library and its always welcoming presence. I wish to acknowledge the sterling efforts of Amanda Campbell, Neil Murray and Helen Ogle in help with the bibliographical and stage history research. I am particularly grateful, as always, to Carole Ebsworth for the analytical skills she has brought to bear on the text as it has evolved; to my daughter, Lydia, for the new eyes she brings to theatrical performances; and to M. Illy for her discovery of previously untrodden ways.

Notes on the Text

A note on the use of quoted texts
I have quietly modernised the quoted seventeenth- and eighteenth-century texts in the interest of accessibility. I have, generally, followed twentieth-century spelling custom and, on occasions, altered punctuation. However, I have left all the important contemporary oaths and archaisms as they were and, in particular, have absolutely not tried to pick up Lord Foppington on his somewhat idiosyncratic use of the English language.

A note on the use of the terms 'Restoration' and 'post-Restoration'
The general description of 'Restoration comedy' has been, and to some extent still is, used as a convenient generic label. I have preferred to write of 'post-Restoration comedy', thus allowing for the possibility of generic connections being made but not stretching unreasonably the notion of 'Restoration' into the eighteenth century.

Vanbrugh and Farquhar in Their Contexts: Histories

1660	Restoration of Charles II. Samuel Pepys starts his diary. Foundation of Royal Society. King's and Duke's Companies given royal patent. First actresses on stage.
1661	New Model Army paid off, and new army established by Charles. Duke's Company at Lincoln's Inn Fields.
1662	Act of Uniformity passed – all ministers refusing new Prayer Book and 39 articles to be deprived of posts. Royal Society incorporated by royal charter. Licensing Act for all publications.
1663	Unsuccessful republican rising in Ireland. Republican unrest in Yorkshire and Durham. First post-Restoration colony founded in Carolina. Royal African Company to trade in slaves, ivory and gold. King's Theatre at Theatre Royal.

1664	V born in London.	Treason trials in north of England. Nell Gwyn joins King's Company.
1665		Second Dutch War. Great Plague. Theatres closed.
1666	V's family move to Chester.	French and Denmark ally with Dutch. Presbyterian uprising defeated in Scotland. Great Fire of London. Theatres reopened in November.
1667	Probable year of F's birth in Londonderry, the son of a Protestant clergyman.	Secret treaty with France. Theatres closed in July for Dutch War.
1668		Betterton and Harris as managers of Duke's Company.
1669		Duke of York converted to Catholicism. Theatres closed to mourn death of Charles's wife, Henrietta-Maria.
1670		Secret Treaty of Dover with France.
1671		New Excise Bill passed. Parliament prorogued after attempts to pass bill to exclude Catholics from office. Dorset Garden Theatre opened.
1672		Third Dutch War. Theatre Royal burnt down.
1673		William of Orange attempts to extract England from war. Test Act passed – all who hold office under the crown or in the army or Royal Navy publicly to repudiate Roman Catholicism.
1674		Parliament reassembled, but prorogued after its attempts to

		disband the standing army, introduce a habeus corpus bill, and further anti-Catholic measures. King's Company at new Drury Lane Theatre.
1675		Cavalier Parliament recalled but prorogued again by end of year. Royal Observatory at Greenwich.
1676		New secret treaty between Charles II and Louis XIV.
1677		Parliament recalled, but again prorogued as part of financial deal with Louis XIV of France. Anglo-Dutch Treaty. Charles Killigrew takes over management of King's Company from Thomas Killigrew.
1678		The Popish Plot. Parliament recalled and prorogued again.
1679		Parliament dissolved and election held. First Exclusion Parliament in attempts to deny Duke of York the succession. Prorogued.
1680		Second Exclusion Parliament.
1681		Charles dissolves Oxford Parliament. Shaftsbury arrested for treason.
1682		United Actor's Company formed by Betterton and Smith after 'revolt'. Monmouth rebellion.
1683	V goes to France to study architecture.	Rye House Plot. Monmouth involved, but pardoned.
1684		Trial of Titus Oates
1685		Charles II dies; theatres closed for

		three months. James II succeeds. Duke of Argyle leads unsuccessful Scottish rising.
1686	V takes commission as Ensign in Lord Huntingdon's regiment, but quickly resigns.	League of Augsburg formed to protect German interests.
1687		James II's first Declaration of Indulgence.
1688	V imprisoned as 'spy' at Calais for his support of William of Orange.	James II flees country.
1689		Accession of William III and Mary. James in Ireland with French troops to support Catholic rebels.
1690		Battle of the Boyne: William's Protestant army defeats James's Catholic forces. Colley Cibber starts acting career.
1691	V moved to Vincennes prison.	Catholic Army defeated at Battle of Aughrim. Treaty of Limerick.
1692	V moved to Bastille, and later freed, returning to England.	French invasion planned. War continues in Europe.
1693		Skipwith and Rich take over United Company.
1694	F at Trinity College, Dublin.	Death of Queen Mary; theatres closed. Bank of England formed.
1695	V Captain of Marines in Lord Berkeley's regiment.	Namur recaptured by army under William. Betterton leads actors to Lincoln's Inn Fields Theatre.
1696	F acting in Smock Alley Company in Dublin. V's	Lord Chancellor to license all plays for performance.

	The Relapse and *Aesop* (Drury Lane).	
1697	F comes to London. V's *Aesop, Part II* (Drury Lane), and *The Provoked Wife* (Lincoln's Inn Fields).	Treaty of Ryswick.
1698	F's *Love and a Bottle* (Drury Lane), and publication of his novella, *Adventures of Covent Garden*. V's *A Short Vindication of* The Relapse *and* The Provoked Wife *from Immorality and Prophaness*. *The Country House* (Drury Lane).	Robert Wilks in Drury Lane Company. Collier's *A Short View of the Immorality and Prophaness of the English Stage*.
1699	F's *The Constant Couple* (Drury Lane). V architect for Castle Howard.	Army Disbanding Act passed despite William's protests.
1700	V's *The Pilgrim* (Drury Lane).	Death of Carlos II begins Spanish Succession crisis.
1701	F's *Sir Harry Wildair* (Drury Lane).	Pretender recognised by Louis XIV; French War.
1702	F's *The Inconstant* and *The Twin Rivals* (Drury Lane), and publication of his *Love and Business*, which included his *Discourse Upon Comedy*. V Comptroller to the Board of Works; *The False Friend* (Drury Lane).	William III dies; Anne succeeds. Marlborough opens campaign in War of Spanish Succession.
1703	F marries Margaret Penell. F's *The Stage Coach* (Drury Lane). V becomes Carlisle Herald; begins work on Queen's Theatre, Haymarket.	Parliament agrees to large increase in size of Marlborough's army.

1704	F lieutenant in army, on recruiting service. V Clarenceux King-at-Arms; (with Congreve and Walsh) *Squire Trelooby* (Lincoln's Inn Fields).	Battle of Blenheim won by Allies in War of Spanish Succession.
1705	V commissioned as architect with Hawksmoor for Blenheim Palace. Manager (with Congreve) of Queen's Theatre; *The Confederacy* and *The Mistake* (Queen's).	Queen's Theatre opened.
1706	F's *The Recruiting Officer* (Drury Lane). V in Hanover as Herald; loosening ties with Queen's Theatre.	Battle of Ramillies won.
1707	F's *The Beaux Stratagem* opens 8 March (Queen's). F dies 29 April. V to restore Kimbolton Castle; *The Cuckold in Conceit* (Queen's).	Act of Union between England and Scotland. Bank of England survives run on its funds.
1708		Two Companies united at Drury Lane. Battle of Oudenarde won.
1709		Thames freezes over. Battle of Malplaquet. Barrier Treaty with Holland.
1710	F's poem *Barcellona* published. V architect for King's Weston.	General election with huge victory for Tories.
1711		South Sea Company formed.
1712		Peace Congress at Utrecht. Stamp Act passed, effectively censoring newspapers.

1713		Lords Oxford and Bolingbroke in struggle for parliamentary control.
1714	V knighted by George I.	Death of Anne; succession of George I.
1715	V architect for Greenwich Hospital.	Whigs win general election. Death of Louis XIV.
1716	V starts work on Eastbury.	Septennial Act.
1717		Start of Mediterranean crisis.
1718	V designs Floors Castle.	Britain and France sign secret convention to ensure Charles VI's commitment to Triple Alliance in return for help in Mediterranean crisis.
1719	V married Henrietta Yarborough; two-volume edition of his *Plays* published.	In series of parliamentary crises, Robert Walpole begins his rise to power.
1720	V architect for Seton Delaval.	South Sea Bubble; first major crisis in new capitalist economy; Walpole able to become first 'prime' minister.
1721	V to restore Audley End.	Walpole raises large loan to calm financial crisis.
1722		Jacobite plot discovered, and Bishop Atterbury arrested. Scandal of Wood's half-pence coinage debasement in Ireland.
1723		Lord Bolingbroke pardoned, and returns to England; sets up *Craftsman* newspaper attacking Walpole, and is at head of extra-parliamentary 'country' opposition to Whig regime. Much of opposition centred on Walpole's

1
Lives, Times and Theatres

At the turn of the seventeenth century, Britain – as it was just about
to become after a century of negotiations[1] – was on the verge of
becoming established as the first great capitalist state. It had had its
revolution, when the last attempt by the monarchy to keep a
stranglehold of power over the increasingly independent Parliament had resulted in Charles I's public execution outside the
Banqueting House, where he had formerly performed in masques.
And, following the Commonwealth period of Oliver and Richard
Cromwell, Charles II had been welcomed back in 1660 to take his
place on the throne. Popular history places a great deal of emphasis
on him as the 'merry monarch', the instigator of long years of
hedonistic revelry. It is a view that was perpetuated by the theatres,
which were officially opened after a series of puritan-inspired laws
prohibiting performances had been passed in the Commonwealth
period; and, in particular, by the comedies, whose celebration of
sexual gratification and aristocratic privilege merely confirmed the
worst fears of the puritan reformers about the dangers of theatrical
licence. There were, and remain, unconfirmed rumours that a
naked production of Lord Rochester's *Sodom* had even been
performed at Court.[2]

In a brief introduction there is a danger of becoming reductive,[3]
but Charles II's reign did have its other side. The struggle with

Parliament was by no means over, and the King's attempts to revive essentially medieval notions of the 'divine right' of the monarchy served rather to hasten the process by which effective rule of the country would move away from 'God's anointed' and towards the 'elected' representatives. Significantly, the most influential work of political theory of the period, Hobbes' *Leviathan* of 1651, was able to be read both as an apologia for Stuart absolutism and as a blueprint for the new world of contract theory, in which monarch and subjects were considered to have bought into an agreement over the terms and limitations of rule that had implications for both parties.

The reign was also plagued by expensive foreign wars, on a scale that created for the first time a 'national debt', a problem that was solved by the formation of the Bank of England, which was given a monopoly of banking activity in return for underwriting that debt. This both further weakened the power of the monarchy and significantly advanced the capitalist interests of the new City world. The puritan movement that had largely provided the ideological underpinning for the English Revolution did not disappear at the time of the Restoration; and its most important public manifestation came in the formation of the Whig interest, the 'rump' of the Revolutionary Party, a grouping that looked to the new monetary world of the City, commerce and trade, as opposed to the Tories, who represented the older values of land and inherited wealth and privilege – a clash that was increasingly on view in the comedies of the late seventeenth century. Puritanism continued to be a dominant force in the wider public arena as well, producing the ground-swell of opposition that would culminate in, amongst other things, the publication of Jeremy Collier's *A Short View of the Immorality and Prophaness of the English Stage* (1698). That Charles should have been seen quite clearly as leaning towards the Catholic interest, both in his private life and in the world of international diplomacy, created further tensions; and, in 1682, he was challenged by the unsuccessful Protestant rebellion led by his own illegitimate son, Monmouth.

Charles died in 1685 and was succeeded by James II, a monarch who was even more public about his Catholicism. The final straw for Parliament came with the birth of a male Catholic heir and, in the face of representations being made to the Protestant House of Orange in the Netherlands, James fled the country and William III was enthroned, with his consort Mary, in the 'Glorious Revolution' of 1688. The removal of a second Stuart monarch in less than 50 years was less bloodily achieved and was legitimised in terms of the by now strongly developed theories of contract, whereby James was judged to have broken the terms of agreement between ruler and ruled. Locke's *Two Treatises of Government*, published two years after the event, was regarded as a vindication of the Glorious Revolution, and further developed the central notion of contract that was to lead to a system of parliamentary rule which, in the eighteenth century, meant that the formation of a parliamentary opposition to His or Her Majesty's government was no longer regarded as a treasonable act, but as an important plank in the move towards parliamentary 'democracy'.

The way in which William III took power reinforced the point, for it was only after quite explicit terms had been agreed on both sides that the invitation to 'invade' was made. Parliament, too, started to come to terms with the notion of a contract between itself and those of the population who were entitled to vote, and administrations had fixed terms with the need to go to the country for elections at regular intervals.

Sir John Vanbrugh and George Farquhar were both born after the Restoration of Charles, and this alone separates them from the earlier generation of post-Restoration playwrights, whose ideological presuppositions were formed in an atmosphere dominated by the issues raised by the Civil War and the Restoration. That they wrote in the shadow of this earlier generation is at least as important as the fact that they were writing in the context of a new kind of society, for they were always modifiers of the tradition rather than theatrical revolutionaries intent on breaking with the past.

Their names are frequently linked despite their very considerable differences. The very fact that they were both writing comedies in the late seventeenth and early eighteenth centuries, and were both conscious of working within the constraints of established theatrical and generic traditions, is in itself a reason for making such a link. Put simply, they are the last two great representatives of that line of theatre that has been generally described as, first, Restoration comedy and, then, the comedy of manners. However, Farquhar's career as a dramatist is actually in stark contrast to that of Vanbrugh. Whilst Vanbrugh aspired to a world of aristocratic privilege, seeing the writing of plays as virtually incidental to his other careers, Farquhar's attitude was straightforwardly economic.

Farquhar wrote to support himself, a point that he is at pains to stress in the Preface to the Reader of his second play, *The Constant Couple* (1699): 'I am very willing to acknowledge the beauties of this play, especially those of the third night', when the author would qualify for royalties. In contrast, if the added Prologue to the third-night performance of his first staged play, *The Relapse* (1696), is to be believed, Vanbrugh donated the usually much sought after benefits to the actors. It is a difference in attitude that crucially defines a separation of economic positions.

George Farquhar was born in Londonderry in 1667 and acted in Dublin with the Smock Alley Company without any great degree of success; this period of his life is perhaps best epitomised by a near disastrous incident in which he drew the actual blood of a fellow actor during a stage fight in a performance of John Dryden's *The Indian Emperor*.[4] According to an early biographer he was encouraged by his fellow actor, and lifelong friend, Robert Wilks to 'quit the stage and write a comedy'. To this end Wilks gave him some small financial assistance, whilst Farquhar wrote a draft of what was to be his first production, *Love and a Bottle*.[5] Shortly afterwards, he arrived in London and the theatre impresario Christopher Rich was persuaded to find a place for it in the 1698 season at the Drury Lane Theatre.

It was at this same theatre that John Vanbrugh's first production had also been staged, two years earlier, but the circumstances of his arrival there are somewhat different. Vanbrugh was born into a large family in 1664. As his name suggests, the family had originated in the Netherlands, his grandfather having come to England as a Protestant refugee in the late 1580s. As a result of the outbreak of the plague in London the family moved to Chester, where they prospered. At the age of 19 Vanbrugh was sent to France, where he remained for about three years, returning to England in 1685, the year of the death of Charles II. The following year he bought a commission in the Earl of Huntingdon's regiment which, in 1688, enthusiastically supported the arrival of the Protestant William of Orange (William III). On the death of his father soon after, Vanbrugh, as the oldest surviving child, received a significant percentage of the family wealth.

By 1688 he was again in France, and was imprisoned as a suspected spy. Despite the best efforts of family and influential friends, it was not until 1692 that he was eventually released, having been moved first from Calais to Vincennes, and thence to the Bastille. It was here that Vanbrugh probably started work on *The Provoked Wife*.[6] Certainly, his extended times in France were to make him far more familiar than Farquhar with Continental drama. For instance, Vanbrugh's *The Confederacy* of 1705 is based on Dancourt's *Les Bourgeoisies à la Mode*, which was first performed in Paris the very month that he was released from the Bastille. Back in England, he was stationed in Dorset near the home of Sir Thomas Skipwith, who was one of the patentees of the Drury Lane Theatre. Offered friendship and patronage by Sir Thomas he produced a play, *The Relapse*, by way of thanks.

Immediately before the first productions by Farquhar and Vanbrugh, there had been only two theatres in London. After the Restoration of Charles II in 1660, theatrical patents had been given to Thomas Killigrew and Sir William D'Avenant to form the King's and the Duke of York's Companies, respectively. Following the Commonwealth period, in which successive Acts of Parliament had effectively brought an end to public theatre, the Dorset Garden Theatre (the Duke's Company) had opened in 1671, and the New Drury Lane Theatre (the King's Company) in 1674. The former theatre was not properly operational until the date of the opening of the second theatre, however, and the Duke's Company had a somewhat chequered existence – a history which is described by Milhouse as one of 'disaster, deceit, theft and dissension'[7] – until its amalgamation with the King's Company, as the United Company, in 1682. The new company was initially successful, largely through the example of its leading actor and theatre manager, Thomas Betterton. In 1687, Charles D'Avenant (Sir William's son) sold out to his brother Alexander, who introduced another brother, Thomas, as manager over the head of Betterton. Sir Thomas Skipwith had put up the money to allow Alexander to take control of the company. Alexander, quickly getting into financial difficulties, was forced to find other investors, including Christopher Rich, before fleeing the country in 1693. At this point Skipwith assumed control of the company and Rich took on its day-to-day management.

Rich's was not a popular regime with the actors, however, for his prime intent was cost-cutting in the cause of increasing the profits. Attempts by the company's actors to get legal redress having failed, in 1695 William III was prevailed upon to allow a licence to be granted to a new company headed by Betterton, and most of the more established players moved with him to Lincoln's Inn Fields. The rebellion was burlesqued in the opening scene of Vanbrugh's *Aesop, Part II*, which was performed at Drury Lane in 1697. The rebel company is pictured as a leaky boat whose crew has unwisely left the security of the good ship *Patent*. The player tells Aesop that the Captain (Betterton) had promised him and the other rebels a new life, but could only offer bread and cheese:

AESOP: I hope he kept his word with them?
PLAYER: That he did; he made the boatswain's mate, lieutenant; he made the cook, doctor: he was forced to be purser, and pilot, and gunner himself; and the swabber took orders to be chaplain.
AESOP: But with such unskilful officers I'm afraid they'll hardly keep above water long.
PLAYER: Why truly, Sir, we care not how soon they are under: but curst folks thrive, I think. I know nothing else that makes them swim. I'm sure, by the rules of navigation, they ought to have over-set long since; for they carry a great deal of sail, and have very little ballast.
AESOP: I'm afraid you ruin one another. I fancy if you were all in a ship together again, you'd have less work and more profit.

(I, i)

Viewed in this light, Vanbrugh's support of Skipwith and the Drury Lane Theatre is not too surprising, though it should be noted that even as these words were being heard on stage Vanbrugh was completing *The Provoked Wife*, which would receive its first performances at the new theatre in Lincoln's Inn Fields. Certainly Betterton's new company had its problems. It had no access to the only two decent theatres in London, and it had left Rich with not only control of Drury Lane and Dorset Gardens but also all the United Company's stock of costumes and scenery. The Lincoln's Inn Fields Theatre had reverted to use as a tennis court in March 1674, when the King's Company moved to the Theatre Royal (rebuilt after a fire in 1672), and it had to be reconverted from scratch.[8] However, although all of Farquhar's plays (with the exception of *The Beaux Stratagem*) premiered at Drury Lane, already, by 1697,

Vanbrugh had allowed *The Provoked Wife* to open at Lincoln's Inn Fields. The open struggle for supremacy between the two companies was to prove costly. If Drury Lane had all the equipment, they had certainly lost most of the best actors. Robert Wilks was persuaded to return to London in 1699 – having briefly performed there in 1693–4 – and in the epilogue written by Farquhar for his first performance after his return to Drury Lane, 'the actor spoke openly of leaving behind his Dublin success for the blandishments of London'.[9]

Suitably enough, Wilks took the lead in Farquhar's next play, *The Constant Couple* of 1699. The play was a triumphant success, establishing both the leading actor and the playwright in London, and it played for an unprecedented 53 nights in the capital that year,[10] a box-office feat not bettered until John Gay's *The Beggar's Opera* of 1728, which went on to become easily the most successful play of the entire eighteenth century. Nothing that Farquhar could do subsequently, until the very end of his career, could match that success, including his attempt at a sequel, *Sir Harry Wildair* (1701), in which Wilks reintroduced the lead character of *The Constant Couple* with a further set of adventures.

Farquhar continued to produce plays for Drury Lane. *The Inconstant* and *The Twin Rivals* (both of 1702) did little to add to his reputation and nothing to add to his pocket. Disillusioned with the results of his efforts and, by 1703, tricked into marriage to an older widow who brought with her not the promised fortune but children by her previous marriage, Farquhar did what many of the penniless heroes of his own plays considered – he took an army commission, during the course of which he acted as a recruiting officer in, amongst other places, Shrewsbury and Lichfield. This too proved to be a bad financial move, and he left the service some time in 1705. From his experiences came the genesis of the first of his two great last plays, *The Recruiting Officer* (1706). In this play the first words spoken by Justice Balance to his future son-in-law, Captain Plume, refer to the contemporary battles being fought by Marlborough on the Continent, in the War of the Spanish Succession, and he refuses to be distracted from his enquiries by any romantic fiddle-faddle of the Captain's:

BALANCE: Look'e, Captain, give us but blood for our money, and you shan't want men. I remember that for some years of

the last war we had no blood or wounds but in the Officers'
mouths; nothing for our millions but newspapers not
worth a reading. Our Armies did nothing but play at prison
bars; but now ye have brought us Colours and Standards
and prisoners. Ods my life, Captain, get us but another
Marshall of France, and I'll go myself for a soldier.

PLUME: Pray, Mr Balance, how does your fair daughter?

BALANCE: Ah! Captain, what is my daughter to a Marshall of
France? We're upon a nobler subject. I want to have a
particular description of the Battle Of Hochstet.

PLUME: The battle, sir, was a very pretty battle as one would
desire to see, but we were all intent so upon victory that we
never minded the battle; all that I know of the matter is,
our General commanded us to beat the French, and we did
so; and if he pleases to say the word, we'll do it again. But
pray, Sir, how goes Miss Silvia?

BALANCE: Still upon Silvia! For shame, Captain, you're engaged
already, wedded to the war. War is your mistress, and it is
below a soldier to think of any other.

(II, i)

Balance's insistent query about the Battle of Hochstet (that is, of
Blenheim) is telling. In August 1704, the allied forces under
Marlborough had defeated the French, and under all the antics to
recruit new soldiers lies not only the glory of this victory but the
'blood' that Balance looks to see; for there were approximately
50,000 casualties upon both sides. Contemporary audiences would
be more likely to see events through Balance's eyes; more recent
theatre-goers perhaps less so.

The Recruiting Officer did much to redeem Farquhar's reputation
but was not sufficient, despite a number of benefit nights, to alter
his financial circumstances. Shortly after this, desperately ill, and
not far off death, Farquhar was by now reduced to penury. He was
visited by his friend Wilks, who found him lodged in a miserable
garret:

Wilks advised him to write a play and that it should be brought
to the stage with all expedition: 'Write,' says Farquhar, 'It is
impossible that a man can write common sense who is heart-
less, and has not a shilling in his pocket.' 'Come George,' replied

Wilks, 'banish melancholy, draw your drama, and I will call on you this day week to see it, but as an empty pocket may cramp your genuis, I desire you will accept of my mite,' and gave him twenty guineas. Mr Farquhar immediately drew up the drama of the Beaux-Stratagem; which he delivered to Mr Wilks, and it was approved of by him and the Managers, and finished in six weeks.[11]

Whether this is a totally reliable account of events or not, the essential circumstances are uncontested. But what is not in doubt is that *The Beaux Stratagem* was an enormous success, both then and through subsequent theatrical history; and that Farquhar did not live to take either the applause or the money that was his due.

Farquhar's last play was the only one of his works not to be premiered at Drury Lane. It opened at the Queen's Theatre in the Haymarket, a new venue which had been designed and built by Vanbrugh and his Whig friends from the Kit-Kat Club. Vanbrugh had stayed loyal to his benefactor, Sir Thomas Skipwith, against Rich's attempts to skim as much profit as possible from Drury Lane, but had already embarked on a second career as an architect, chiefly through the patronage of Charles Howard, the Earl of Carlisle, for whom he designed Castle Howard. One of Vanbrugh's fellow members of the Kit-Kat Club was the playwright William Congreve, and the two of them successfully applied to Queen Anne for a licence to run a new playhouse. The capital for the project was raised by subscriptions from patrons, who were promised free passes to the theatre.

The Queen's Theatre opened in April 1705 with a production of Geber's *The Loves of Ergasto*, an example of the craze for Italian opera which the new theatre was primarily intent on servicing. The production was a disaster, and the interior was felt generally to be too extravagant for the purpose. The theatre:

> was much too large. Vanbrugh's grandiose ideas of vast triumphal pieces of architecture as a venue for singers and actors, and a splendid setting for the Quality watching them, had ignored the small details of theatre planning.[12]

It was, from the moment of its inception, the subject of considerable controversy, not least for Vanbrugh's choice of location. It was

surrounded by fields and anticipated by some years the fashionable
development of the West End of London. Furthermore, the chosen
site had formerly been a stable-yard, a fact that proved irresistible to
praisers and detractors alike. The poet Samuel Garth enthused:

> Majestic columns stand where dunghills lay.
> And cars triumphal rise from bales of hay.

Whilst Defoe attacked it:

> A lay-stall this, Apollo spoke the word.
> And straight arose a Playhouse from a turd.[13]

From the outset the venture was beset with financial problems,
and by 1708 the situation was desperate. Vanbrugh, by now well in
with Court circles (and, in particular, with the Marlboroughs),
sought patronage from Lord Manchester, who was, suitably in view
of Vanbrugh's continued enthusiasm for promoting Italian opera,
the ambassador to Venice. Vanbrugh had briefly given over control
of the new theatre, but then turned to Owen Swinney, who subsequently gained the ascendance.[14]

By this time, Vanbrugh's career as a playwright was effectively
over. His two early triumphs, *The Relapse* (1696) and *The Provoked
Wife* (1697), were already a somewhat distant memory to the public,
and the rest of his writing career was devoted to adaptations.
However, the first of his last three plays to be performed at the
Queen's Theatre, *The Confederacy*, has a power and a contemporary
immediacy that demonstrated that he could still manage the thing.
Subsequently, Vanbrugh would concentrate his efforts on archi-
tecture and on politics. In 1703 he had used the good services of his
benefactor, Charles Howard, to become Carlisle Herald, an ap-
pointment which paved the way to him becoming Clarenceux
King-at-Arms in 1704 (the day before his potboiler, *Squire Trelooby*,
opened at Lincoln's Inn Fields).

In 1719 Vanbrugh married Henrietta Yarborough, who was
nearly 30 years younger than him, and, although he again became
involved with the running of the theatre at the Haymarket in the
early 1720s, he was by then more intent on using his reputation as
an architect and his contacts with the great and the powerful to
acquire more architectural commissions. His friendship with the

Duke and Duchess of Marlborough was of key importance, so that when a grateful nation decided to bestow the hero of the Wars of the Spanish Succession with a palace it was, not surprisingly, Vanbrugh who was, in 1705, engaged to undertake the work. It is a minor irony that Farquhar should have written his greatest play, *The Recruiting Officer*, in the shadow of the Battle of Blenheim, whilst it fell to Vanbrugh to honour the event with Blenheim Palace. The following year, Vanbrugh was sent as a herald to the Court of Hanover, as part of the preparation for the accession of George I, by whom he was gratefully knighted in 1714. His subsequent career was spent largely as an architect and when he died, in 1726, the worlds of the two playwrights whose names have become historically entwined, Vanbrugh and Farquhar, could scarcely have been further apart. But, as we shall see, their plays proclaim the terms of this difference.

2
At Play

A knowledgeable audience accustomed to attending the sort of theatre that still characterises London's Shaftesbury Avenue today would probably recognise it as, in many ways, a perpetuation of the kind of theatre in which Vanbrugh and Farquhar's plays were produced on the edge of the seventeenth and eighteenth centuries. However, an audience magically transported from an original performance of, say, *The Relapse* to a contemporary revival would face far greater difficulties in establishing the connection. For, although much of the essential structure of the auditorium and performance area might appear related, virtually everything that takes place in a modern theatre – from the style of, and the technical aids to, performance to the constituency and behaviour of the audience – would be quite alien.

It is important to stress this since, effectively, the period I will be considering in this book sees the beginning of the evolution of modern mainstream theatre. Many of the now familiar components were already in place, a fact that makes it the more vital to understand the different way in which they were in place. The proscenium was by now an established framing device for the action, and that action was to move increasingly within the defined area of that stage-box, a move that was best exemplified by Christopher Rich's cutting of the fore-stage at Drury Lane towards the turn of the century. But it was a move that was prompted anyway by the greater significance being given to the representation of location.

After the Restoration, patents were given to Thomas Killigrew and William D'Avenant to form the King's and the Duke's Company. The theatres they used were converted real tennis courts and, although we know little in detail about the actual organisation of these theatres, the one major difference between the two was the emphasis that D'Avenant placed on the use of scenic devices.[1] As a result of the obvious audience interest in the increasing sophistication of scenic locations, when the two new theatres were built, Dorset Garden in 1671 (for the Duke's Men) and the new Theatre Royal, Drury Lane, in 1674 (for the King's Men), although both possessed a fore-stage area projecting about 20 feet into the pit area, they were also equipped to offer their audiences a series of scenic backgrounds against which the action could be played.

A backdrop would be permanently in position throughout the performance – a backdrop that would be used over and over again for different plays. Changes of scene could be indicated by the placement of movable flats, which would be slid into position on fixed grooves. In front of these were positioned a series of side flats and hinged wings, offering a crude sense of perspective and, on occasion, locations in which actors might be hidden or discovered. The doors in the proscenium were used not only for entrances and exits, but for the same purposes of hiding and disclosure, and each would have a balcony above, adding further to the playing area.[2]

It is thus entirely possible to look from these theatres, through the Georgian model, to present-day Shaftesbury Avenue; but really only with the advantage of hindsight. Southern has described it as 'scenery in the stage sense of the decking of the stage, but not scenery in the landscape sense of a background seen behind people'.[3] This, in turn, affected the way in which the stage conventions of the time were developed, for no real effects of illusion could be attempted. A stage door that had seen the entrance of a jealous husband might, in the next play, serve as the door to a closet used as a hiding place for a would-be lover.

In his *Restoration Comedy in Performance*, Styan lays emphasis on the way in which, despite the possibilities offered by the kind of machinery I have mentioned above, the change of scene was often indicated by the bringing on or removal of – in full view of the audience – objects which would establish the particular locale; or simply by verbal suggestion, in a way that would have been only too familiar to an audience at Shakespeare's Globe Theatre:

> Speed was of the essence, but the need to bring on clumsy props like tables and chairs no doubt determined that the groove-and-shutter technique would survive for some years before drop-curtains and flying scenery came into use. It is fair to conclude that the chief virtue of the Restoration discovery was not scenic at all, but one of sustaining continuity and pace – a desirable quality in farce and light entertainment.[4]

Nor would the theatres have had much in the way of sophisticated sound or lighting effects. The number of songs offered by one of the two male leads, Archer, in *The Beaux Stratagem* might alert us to the very frequent use of an orchestra, as might the common use of a dance, signifying harmony at the end of so many plays – and, equally, might suggest reasons why Vanbrugh's new theatre, the Queen's in the Haymarket, was originally designed to take advantage of the new vogue for operas; but little was to be expected in the way of what we would now describe as sound effects. Storms could be created to some extent orally, but a theatre whose performances were seen by the daytime light through its windows with additional illumination from suspended chandeliers could do little to heighten the effect. The use of candles to indicate a night scene – indeed, usually a bedchamber scene – would have been little more than symbolic, even with the presence of additional candles in the deep-stage wings.

However, these aspects of performance are in a sense at the periphery of the difference between theatre then and now. The history of performance is, after all, really only the history of its changing conventions. It is not until we consider the overall context in which performance took place and, in particular, the peculiar proximity of the action on stage and that in the auditorium that the size of the historical gap begins to be apparent.

Half-way through Farquhar's *The Constant Couple* (1699) and its complicated unravelling of a plot that will eventually reveal that Colonel Standard and Lady Lurewell are long-parted lovers, the Colonel bursts into his future wife's house. The pair enter on a lively bout of mutual recriminations. Lady Lurewell's tactic (and given her name, not surprisingly so) is to lie; Colonel Standard's (and given his name, not surprisingly so) is to confront her with the truth as he sees it: 'First, your heart is false, your eyes are double; one look belies another; and then your tongue does contradict them all'. In an aside to the audience, the lady admits that he is in the right, before attempting a new tack:

> LUREWELL: Hold, sir, you have got the playhouse cant upon your tongue and think that wit may privilege your railing; but I must tell you, sir, that what is satire upon the stage, is ill manners here.
> STANDARD: What is feigned upon the stage, is here in reality real falsehood.

The conjunction is a familiar one, of course, and has stood playwrights in good stead from Shakespeare through to Stoppard; but its particular use here helps raise questions that are crucial to the kind of theatre that Farquhar and Vanbrugh found themselves writing for towards the end of the seventeenth century. In part, the dialogue serves to indicate the difference in the roles being played by the Colonel and his lady. Lurewell is in every possible way a part of the playhouse world. She is an intriguing flirt who uses all means at her disposal to take revenge on the male sex, which she feels has wronged her. Immediately after the dialogue above she persuades the Colonel that he has not actually seen his rival in attendance – 'you're dreaming.... Will you open your eyes, now that I have rubbed them open?' – and it is left to him to conclude, 'Nay, then there is no certainty in Nature; and truth is only falsehood well disguised' (III, v).

The Colonel seeks to operate in what is for him a real world, of nature, of honesty and of morality, and finds himself increasingly drawn into a plot that is not only taking place in a theatre but is *of* that theatre. His attempt to make a distinction between that which is 'feigned upon the stage' and that which is 'here [in the world outside the theatre] in reality real falsehood' has, then, a double-edged significance. For, in the period immediately preceding Farquhar's first stage efforts, the distinction was never more problematic.

In the Restoration and immediate post-Restoration period the link between the social worlds depicted in the comedies on stage and those enacted by the audiences that flocked to see them was more intense than at any other period in British theatre history. Later critics have derived almost as much pleasure as Sir George Etherege's contemporaries would have done in attempting to identify the stage characters of his *The Man of Mode* (1676) as counterparts of the London world in which they operated. And, although the invitation to make such attempts at identification is not unusual in itself, the comedies of the post-Restoration period derived a great deal of their fascination for their audiences from the fact that it is virtually impossible to draw a line between the social worlds of the characters on stage and those of the various audiences.

There is still considerable controversy about the exact nature of post-Restoration audiences – and certainly by the time that Vanbrugh and Farquhar were writing they consisted of a far wider spectrum of society than in earlier years – but it is evident that in the period from the Restoration until the accession of William and Mary (1660–89) the major proportion of the theatre income derived from those sections of the audience who would not only relate directly to the characters depicted on stage, but saw in their plots and intrigues little more than an extension of those of their own lives of leisured activity, albeit frequently in terms that were alternatively heightened or satirised.

Indeed, some years later, it was a central part of Vanbrugh's attempt to refute the allegations of immorality levelled at his work that he simply wrote what he saw. He talks of the stage as a 'glass for the world to view itself in; people ought therefore to see themselves as they are; if it makes their faces too fair, they won't know they are dirty, and by consequence will neglect to wash 'em'.[5] The latter part of this explanation, that the writing has the intention of reforming, is a familiar one, and can be found in Ben Jonson as it can in Jonathan Swift, who prefaced his *Battle of the Books* (1697) with a more honestly cynical rationale: 'Satire is a sort of glass, wherein beholders do generally discover everybody's face but their own; which is the chief reason for that kind of reception it meets in the world, and that so very few are offended with it'.[6] I am less concerned here with the apologia – though, of course, that too has its part to play in the workings of the contemporary theatre – than with the connection made between the world inside and outside the theatre. Not every male member of the audience lived a life even approaching that according to the hedonistic tenets of a Lord Rochester – no more than did the characters in the plays – but the patterns of behaviour were imprinted firmly on the social, and the fantasised, lives of the spectators.

What this means is that there was a direct connection between the scenes depicted on stage, which move between the rooms (both public and private) of the beau monde, the taverns which provided a location for the male audience's adventures, and the parks which offered a neutral territory where ladies, as securely masked as their counterparts in the plays, might freely consort with gentlemen acquaintances. But, more importantly, this connection between stage events and social reality meant that the theatre itself must be thought of in a way that redefines the sense of it as offering a clear separation between a performed spectacle and an audience gathered to respond to the spectacle. The lines of demarcation were less apparent, the connection between performers and audience more intimate; this is evidenced, for instance, by the heightened use of the aside in post-Restoration comedy; and it is made physically more apparent after about 1690 with the reintroduction of seating on stage 'from the orchestra half-way to the back-scene'.[7]

The theatre was not only a place to observe a depiction of social life on stage – it was itself uniquely a part of that social life. At the beginning of *The Man of Mode*, Medley tells Dorimant that he is aware of his assignations with 'a Vizard at the Playhouse'. Medley wonders how his mistress, Mrs Loveit, will respond if she finds out, and his friend tells him, 'this mask, for a farther confirmation of what I have been these two days swearing to her, made me yesterday at the Playhouse make her a promise before her face, utterly to break off with Loveit' (I, i).

The deployment of masks by ladies attending the theatre makes any distinction between mistress (with an implication of rank or status) and whore (with an implication of lack or rank or status) difficult; but it is entirely characteristic of the period that Dorimant should be using the theatre in this way. It was a meeting place for the two sexes, and one – like the parks – that allowed men to meet with women associated with both the private houses and the taverns. The wearing of masks became such a moral issue that the practice was banned by Queen Anne, and the playbill for Vanbrugh's *The Country House* (1703) declared that no one would be admitted if wearing one.[8]

It is dangerous to take assertions from the plays at face value, but much less so than many earlier critics have alleged. The comedies are so preoccupied with self-referential details about the theatre and its audiences – including the frequent complaint in prologues of the inattention paid to the plays by their restive and talkative patrons – that, even allowing for exaggeration, a reliable depiction emerges. Sir Novelty Fashion's own account, in Colley Cibber's *Love's Last Shift* (1696), of his particular delight at there being now two theatres in which to be seen clearly owes as much to direct observation as it does to heightened satire. He attempts to seduce Narcissa by talking only of his own qualities. When she protests that he has yet to mention her, his response is telling:

> FASHION: I'll come to you presently, madam, I have just done: then you must know, my coach and equipage are as well known as myself; and since the conveniency of two play houses, I have a better opportunity of showing them; for between every act – whisk – I am gone from one to th'other: oh what pleasure 'tis, at a good play, to get out before half an act's done.
>
> NARCISSA: Why at a good play?
>
> FASHION: O, madam, it looks particular, and gives the whole audience an opportunity of turning upon me at once: then do they conclude I have some extraordinary business, or a fine woman to go to at least: and then again, it shows my contempt of what the dull town think their chief diversion: but if I do stay a play out, I always sit with my back to the stage.
>
> NARCISSA: Why so, sir?
>
> FASHION: Then every one will imagine that I have been tired with it before; or that I am jealous who talks to who in the king's box.
>
> (II)

The theatre then both provided a meeting place and reflected in the plots of its comedies heightened accounts of the events attendant on those meetings. In 1702, Farquhar described the consequences in terms of a struggle for supremacy between the action on stage and the behaviour of the audience supposedly present to follow it. When bored, the writer observed, the audience would 'betake themselves to other work; not meeting the diversion they expected on the stage, they shift for themselves in the pit; every one turns about to his neighbour in a mask, and for default of entertainment now, they strike up far more diverting scenes when the play is done'. The result, it is suggested, is far more lewdness than in any play attacked by Collier and the reformers.[9]

In Vanbrugh's *The Relapse* (1696), Loveless attempts to encourage his wife Amanda with the attractions a return to London might have, despite the attendant moral dangers. His conjuring with the pleasures of the playhouse proves a dubious one for his partner:

> LOVELESS: There are delights, of which a private life [in the country] is destitute, which may divert an honest man, and be a harmless entertainment to a virtuous woman. The conversation of the town is one; and truly, with some small allowances, the plays, I think, may be esteemed another.
> AMANDA: The plays, I must confess, have some small charms, and would have more, would they restrain that loose obscene encouragement to vice, which shocks, if not the virtue of some women, at least the modesty of all.
>
> (II, i)

Indeed, as we are about to learn, it was at the theatre that Loveless had recently exchanged glances with the woman whose affair with him will give *The Relapse* its title. In such ways the distinction between the domains of the performers and of the audience is continually opened to question. And if the plays could be relied on to emphasise the fact of their placement in the social context of the theatre, equally they would provide a frequent reminder of the connection between the roles being played by both performers and audience in the spectacle that was involved in their coming together.

At the beginning of *Love's Last Shift*, the play to which Vanbrugh had written *The Relapse* as a sequel, the servant Snap tells his master, that same Loveless, that his wife was so attractive that she was 'more talked of than a good actress with a maidenhead' (I, i). That Loveless's wife, the patient, virtuous and faithful Amanda, was being played by an actress gives such remarks a double edge; for, to audiences at the plays, the separation between actress and whore was not only perceived as somewhat vague, but was quite

deliberately kept so by male managements well aware of the pulling
power of a little carefully displayed female flesh. So, later in the
play, Amanda, intent on playing the supposed whore to her husband in order to win him back, is given a stage direction by Cibber
that makes its point quite explicitly: 'Enter Amanda loosely dressed'.
At the very point in the play where the heroine is about to effect a
miraculous reformation of her husband's behaviour, the audience is
voyeuristically allowed a quite different insight into the activities on
stage.

Elsewhere it is notable how frequently a scene is located in a
bedroom with one or more women dressed in night attire; and
generally, much stress was laid on the sexual attractions of the
actresses. As Simon Callow has advised contemporary counterparts:
'cleavage is a necessity. The 17th century silhouette wasn't achieved
without artifice. Never be ashamed to heave and pad'.[10]

It is difficult to overstress the importance of both the presence of
women on stage in post-Restoration theatre and the way in which
they were used. That many an actress actually found favour, and
even occasionally marriage, with a well connected member of the
audience was true, but more significant was the illusion of availa-
bility. The backstage area was frequently visited by male members
of the audience, sometimes actually during performances. One of
the most obvious points of connection between performers and
audience came with the prologues and epilogues to the plays, the
numbers of which proliferated towards the end of the century. It is
notable how often these direct addresses to the audience, with their
appeals for a sympathetic response, were given to actresses, many
of whom were quite young girls, to perform. Milhous comments: 'A
remarkable number of epilogues delivered by female members of
both companies held out the fairly explicit, if teasing, promise of
sexual favours in return for approval of a play'.[11]

Nor was this deployment of actresses confined to their roles as
females in the plays. For instance, the part of Young Fashion in *The
Relapse* was originally played by an actress, Mary Kent, a fact which
gives a quite different reading of the frequent attempts by Coupler,
the first fully realised homosexual male to grace the English stage, to
busy himself with getting his hands into the supposedly male
character's clothing.

The presence of women on stage dates from the establishment of
the two theatres after the Restoration, and specifically from Charles

II's royal patent of 1660, and clearly the introduction had a momentous effect on the development of English drama. My point here is that it had an equally momentous effect on the social parameters of behaviour in the theatre at large. The fact that, for the first time, men and women were permitted to appear together on the public stage obviously opened up the potential areas of debate about sexual relationships, the over-riding preoccupation of all the comedies; that they did so in the context of theatres whose patrons were themselves in effect a part of the stage action makes the changing nature of those debates all the more fascinating.

To talk as I have so far is to see the performances from an essentially masculine perspective, and a particular version of the masculine at that. And indeed the way in which the plots and characterisation of the plays are formed encourages the construction of such a perspective. Three hundred years after the first performance of the plays I will be discussing, the terms of reference of such a construction are evidently far more problematic. In his remarks about playing *The Relapse* today, Simon Callow, after claiming that the post-Restoration comedies celebrated femininity, is forced to qualify his remark:

> The transformation in sexual politics has called into question the very notion of celebrating femininity: is it not merely another form of oppression, by which women are obliged to behave according to men's definition, satisfying men's fantasies and requirements? This is a very new development, and carries with it, as usual in any ideological breakthrough, a complex mix of gains and losses. What is certain, though, is that the dramatists of the Restoration, both men and women, were far from being feminists. In order to play their characters and understand their plays, we have to take into account the context in which both existed, and one of the more central ingredients was a much more dangerous sort of sexual by-play than had hitherto been seen on the English stage; and central to that was the frisson caused by the arrival of women with all their erotic potential into a hitherto all-male enclave.[12]

However, the situation is actually more complicated than this. To talk of the post-Restoration period as a seamless one in terms of the theatre is misleading. Just as the very fact of women playing

themselves led to changes in that presentation, so the fact that they
were being watched from the audience by other women further
promoted change. Amanda in *The Relapse* was not alone in worrying
about the way in which marriage and adultery were presented on
the stage. As early as 1675 there is evidence of specifically female
opposition to the depiction of their gender and, as Collier acknowledges in his *Short View*, the influence of the 'ladies' began to
effect a change in dramatic sensibility long before his attack was
published.[13]

And this too is but a part of a larger change in the social composition of the audiences. The seating arrangements, and their
pricing, enforced the niceties of social distinction but, according to
Sir Novelty Fashion in Cibber's *Love's Last Shift*, this sense of
division was becoming less acute by the end of the century: 'for the
devil take me, the women of the town now come down so low, that
my very footman, while he kept my place t'other day at the playhouse, carried a mask out of the side-box with him, and, stop my
vitals, the rogue is now taking physic for't' (V, iii). His surprise is as
much at the fact that the prostitute should be sitting in a side box as
that his servant should be able to impose upon her. About a year
later the manager of the Drury Lane Theatre, Christopher Rich,
started to let footmen into the upper gallery gratis, presumably with
the intention of encouraging their employers' attendance, a practice
condemned by Cibber as 'the greatest Plague that ever Play-house
had to complain of'.[14]

The comparative exclusivity of the theatre as it had been recon-
stituted after 1660 was increasingly under threat as new audiences,
a product of the changing society, began to see the theatre as a
possible social location. The political geography of the theatre was
still in place, with its careful placement of different classes of that
society; but the class range was widening and the absolute certainties of the divisions were more in question. All these aspects find
their place in an anonymous account of 1699:

> In our Playhouses of London, besides an Upper-Gallery for
> footmen, coachmen, mendicants, etc, we have three other
> different and distinct classes; the first is called the Boxes, where
> there is one peculiar to the King and Royal Family, and the rest
> for the persons of quality, and for the ladies and gentlemen of
> the highest rank, unless some fools that have more wit than

money, or perhaps more impudence than both, crowd in among 'em. The second is called the Pit, where sit the judges, wits, and censurers.... 'Tis no matter whether it be good or bad, but 'tis a play ... and must be damned. In common with these sit the squires, sharpers, beaus, bullies and whores, and here and there an extravagant male and female Cit. The third is distinguished by the title of the Middle Gallery, where the citizens' wives and daughters, together with the Abigails, servingmen, journeymen and apprentices take their places; and now and then some disponding mistresses and superannuated poets.[15]

The writer is evidently as concerned with social satire as with direct observation, but the terms of the satire are revealing. As the century came to an end, the model of social distinctions offered by the playhouse grew increasingly more fluid. The audiences changed in the range of their social composition and in the more relaxed mobility of the seating arrangements. Money, as the writer indicates, was a great social leveller, a point made rather earlier by, amongst many others, Etherege in *The Man of Mode; Or, Sir Fopling Flutter*, which pits the beau of the old order, Dorimant, against the nouveau riche fop of the play's subtitle, both vying for supremacy on the same stage.

And as the audiences changed, so did the plays they came to see. Why this should be, and its implications, will be the theme of the rest of this book. In his *The Comedy of Manners*, John Palmer summed up the relationship of the work of Vanbrugh and Farquhar to the dramatic models they had inherited: 'Vanbrugh is a dramatist of the fall. He accepted a tradition and shattered it ... Vanbrugh made the breach whereby Farquhar entered in and destroyed the citadel'.[16] This is an overwrought metaphor but it contains within it an important truth. The two playwrights may, in the past, have been subsumed into a conveniently labelled genre of 'Restoration comedy' or the 'comedy of manners' – and certainly they must be linked to the tradition they inherited – but they are writing in a different historical period to their predecessors, and the strains resultant on the attempts to reconcile themselves to past, present and, in Farquhar's case at least, the future are some of the major reasons for their continuing significance as playwrights. In the next chapter I will look at the source of these tensions and consider in some detail one play of the 'new order', Colley Cibber's *Love's Last Shift*, a work that not only sums up well the problematics of the new theatrical sensibility but can be seen quite directly to have kick started the career of the more backward-looking of my two writers, Sir John Vanbrugh.

3
The Moral Reform Movement, *Love's Last Shift* and Changing Sensibilities

Theatre in the period immediately after the Restoration was strongly supported by Charles II and his Court. The two men, Killigrew and D'Avenant, who were awarded the new theatrical patents had been exiled in France with Charles, and the titles of the companies they formed, the King's and the Duke's, bore testament to the strong links. It is no surprise, then, that the plays that were performed by these companies reflected the values of the world of the Court and its environs. But they did so in ways that are more complicated than is now generally perceived for this period of theatrical history. We are now accustomed to thinking of the period almost entirely in terms of its comedies, but the variety of theatrical models on offer was initially much wider than that, and indeed the play with which D'Avenant introduced his Duke's Company, *The Siege of Rhodes* (1661), was the first of many heroic plays of the period, a form of drama described by Harbage as being preoccupied with a notion of virtue that was 'purely aristocratic, limiting the quality to the traits of epic heroes: physical courage, prowess in arms, magnanimity, and fidelity to a code of personal honour'.[1]

This description would fit ill with, say, the antics of Horner in Wycherley's *The Country Wife* (1675), a man who has his impotence proclaimed abroad that he may the more safely seduce the married women of the town without arousing their husbands' suspicions. It is a useful, if somewhat absurd, comparison, for it helps to explain why it is that we now ascribe a different kind of significance to the comedies of the period than to the tragedies and heroic dramas. Where the heroic plays sought to advance a notion of the positive ideals associated with the newly restored monarchy and the aristocracy that immediately surrounded it, the comedies took as their subject not life as, perhaps, it *ought* to be, but life as it *was*. If they offered a celebration of the Restoration, it was in terms of its hedonism, its sensuality and its brilliance. Whether or not it was always a very accurate depiction of the society is, in this context, irrelevant; it seemed more relevant and more attractive to successive generations of audience. Frequently, and often as a defence, the claim was made that the depiction was satirical, with the intention of inculcating reform. Again, this is not a matter of immediate moment; but before long it would be of immense importance.

Heroic plays and tragedies looked backwards to an anyway extremely idealised notion of feudal values, such as might have been found in the days of King Arthur's round table perhaps. That they are no longer in favour today is not simply a question of a difference in aesthetic judgement – although it is certainly also that – but a part of their own history. The further the theatre got from the Restoration of 1660, the more the comedies began to predominate over the more serious fare. Laura Brown traces the decline of the heroic:

> The heroic action evolves from a rigid, straightforward, aesthetically simple, and ideologically sanguine version of the form to an increasingly problematic and complex one. In early heroic plays ... the governing aristocratic code is explicit and unambiguous. Character and conflict are shaped directly by a clear evaluative hierarchy that is rigidly and unvaryingly enacted in every episode of the plot. These plays automatically reproduce a social ideal whose primary political premise is royalist and whose central aesthetic quality is the elaboration of a self-consciously elevated, elitist, or baroque manner.... When the complexity outweighs the efficacy of the standards, and the evaluative hierarchy becomes arbitrary or meaningless ... the form has reached the end of the period of its generic priority.

Heroic plays, like neo-classical epics, continue to be written in the late Restoration and early eighteenth century, but such works are historical anachronisms, no longer central participants in the development of their genre.[2]

It is not that there were not complexities in the comedies, but rather that these complexities reflected the actual problematics of their age and not those of an irreconcilable gap between the ideal and the perceived realities. The increasing dominance of the comedies on the stage was also a result, then, of the changing nature of post-Restoration society and of its theatrical audiences. In considering the way in which the comedies developed, it is vital not only to consider those changes in society at large and in the audience constituencies, but to realise that the two are frequently, and importantly, separable.

Theatre audiences in the post-Restoration period can never be thought of as representative. They may, certainly, have been more dominated by courtly patrons in the early period than they were by the turn of the century, but we are always talking of a fairly small percentage of the population, not even of the nation as a whole but of those who lived in, or had access to, London. Few plays had long runs and, whilst revivals were common, at any one point in time there would have been a small theatre-going pool. Dorset Garden might have held 1200 customers, the new Drury Lane 500–1000, and Lincoln's Inn Fields 400–600.[3] The death of Charles II, and the loss of royal patronage, reduced the money available for productions and, presumably, the number of people attending, and we know that, by the period I will be considering in this book, neither William III nor Anne displayed much other than a critical attitude towards theatrical performance. Equally, we know that theatre audiences were more representative of society as a whole in 1700 than in 1661, but it is not a revolutionary difference.

The instigations for change came from without rather than within the theatre; in this they are genuinely more representative of the larger changes in society, and, in particular, of the increasing influence and power of the newly enriched elements of society, elements whose natural environment might be thought of as the City and not the Court. Historically, the momentum for change has always been associated with the publication of Jeremy Collier's *A Short View of the Immorality and Prophaneness of the English Stage* of

1698. Collier was an unlikely champion to be thrown up on behalf of a puritan moral backlash against the excesses of the stage. He was a Jacobite Catholic and a non-juror, that is to say, a man who, having already sworn allegiance to James II, refused to be sworn again for William III in 1689. Having earlier been imprisoned for his political leanings, he had been outlawed as a result of absolving two men who had plotted to kill William in 1696, a King who by then was firmly established as the Protestant hero of the Battle of the Boyne (1690).

Collier's *Short View* was a vitriolic attack on the blasphemies and licentiousness of the contemporary comedies, most significant for the detailed and illustrated accounts of it that he drew from the plays. Two of the playwrights who were attacked felt moved, in 1698, to publish defences of their work: William Congreve in his *Amendments of Mr Collier's False and Imperfect Citations* and Vanbrugh in his *A Short Vindication of* The Relapse *and* The Provoked Wife *from Immorality and Prophaneness.* Collier's reaction to these counterblasts was swift. In 1699, now riding on a wave of public and royal popularity – the charges against him having been dropped at the monarch's instigation – he published *A Defence of the* Short View *of the Immorality and Prophaneness of the English Stage.* The first 96 pages were devoted almost entirely to Congreve, and a further 42 pages to Vanbrugh.

The opening sentence of Collier's original attack declared, 'The business of plays is to recommend virtue, and discountenance vice', and in his *Short Vindication* Vanbrugh continually protests that this is just his intention: 'what I have done is in general a discouragement to vice and folly; I am sure I intended it, and I hope I have performed it'.[4] His continual rejoinder is that, yes, he has written as Collier says he has, but if he has found 'offensive language', immodest ladies, successful libertines, cuckolding wives, pimps, and the like, it is because they are there to be found, in life. In his anonymously published *The Adventures of Covent Garden* (1699), Farquhar was probably in the right when he had his group of playgoers conclude, 'That the best way of answering Mr Collier was not to have replied at all', although his rider was evidently not true, 'for there was so much fire in his book, had not his adversaries thrown in fuel, it would have fed upon itself, and so have gone out in a blaze'.[5]

The reason why Collier's attack would not have 'gone out in a blaze' is that, although he has become almost solely associated with the backlash against the stage, he was in truth by no means the only person to launch such attacks, and certainly not the initiator of them. He caught the public mood and did not create it. In his *Critical Edition* of Collier's work of 1987, Hellinger identifies the roots of this backlash some two decades earlier,[6] and scholars are now generally in agreement that the *Short View* represented the very public tip of what was by then an extremely large iceberg; for instance, Milhous says: 'the Collier crisis was the climax of nearly two decades of change and protest'.[7]

That Collier's attack should have proved so popular demonstrates that there was already a strong puritan distaste for the excesses of a theatre that was identified, rightly or wrongly, with the celebration of the hedonistic activities associated with, and thus protected by, the Court of King Charles. Public taste, even amongst theatre audiences, was changing before Collier's attack, and the subsequent activities of organisations such as the Society for Reformation of Manners created an umbrella for the utterance of such demands for change. So, it was not that there had not been signs of a puritan opposition to the post-Restoration theatrical celebration of excess before this time; rather that with the accession of William and Mary, and thus the removal of the previous Stuart royal patronage, it became a less problematic public utterance. Shortly after the accession a royal proclamation against immorality was published, and many more were to follow.[8] It was a movement strongly connected with the growth of a pro-Whig mercantile class whose roots lay in the English Revolution, and whose interests in the new world of money and commerce did nothing to undermine their hostility to the old world of aristocratic privilege. For there can be no doubt that it would be more sensible to see the opposition to the theatre as a symbol of an essentially political opposition than as a somehow purely moral one. Indeed, Farquhar makes the connection quite explicitly in *The Constant Couple*, first performed the year after Collier's *Short View* was published, where he has the 'old Merchant' Smuggler, the representative of a corrupt City world, 'reveal' that the attack had been paid for by City money: ''Tis a hard matter now, that an honest sober man can't sin in private for this plaguey stage. I gave an honest Gentleman five guineas myself towards writing a book against it, and it has done no good' (V, ii).

As late as 1702, in his Preface to the published text of *The Twin Rivals*, Farquhar is intent on disputing the terms of Collier's argument, at least as far as *his* theatre audiences were concerned:

The success and countenance that debauchery has met with in plays, was the most severe and reasonable charge against their authors in Mr Collier's *Short View*; and indeed the gentleman had done the drama considerable service, had he arraigned the stage only to punish its misdemeanours, and not to take away its life; but there is an advantage to be made sometimes of the advice of an enemy, and the only way to disappoint his designs, is to improve upon his invective, and to make the stage flourish by virtue of that satire, by which he thought to suppress it. I have therefore in this piece endeavoured to show that an English Comedy may answer the strictness of poetical justice.... And this I take to be one reason that the Galleries were so thin during the run of this play. I thought indeed to have soothed the splenetic zeal of the City by making a Gentleman a Knave and punishing their great grievance – a Whoremaster; but a certain virtuoso of that fraternity has told me since, that the Citizens were never more disappointed, for (said he) however pious we may appear to be at home, yet we never go to that end of the town, but with an intention to be lewd.[9]

Farquhar's playful sense of the importance of class antagonism is noteworthy, as he carefully talks of that City part of the audience located in the gallery and its ideological interests as directly connected with the movement associated with Collier.

The tide of reaction looked unstoppable at the time. Bahlman says that 'The phrase "reformation of manners" appeared everywhere' in the 1690s,[10] and it is clear that the theatre could no longer afford to ignore the growing swell of opposition to it. In January 1696 the Lord Chancellor had issued an order that all plays be fully licensed – that is to say, vetted for approval before performance – and by 1699, the poet laureate Nahum Tate put forward a *Proposal for Regulating the Stage and Stage-Players*, a work written with a clear belief that a total ban on the theatres was being considered if such reforms did not occur.[11]

The reform movement was, then, directly to affect the way in which new plays modified the dramatic traditions, and it also provided the inspiration for a new form of drama, the sentimental comedy, in which the excesses of the post-Restoration tradition were excised and a morally correct happy ending was provided in a way that actually began to bring in new elements to the audiences.

Sir Richard Steele, the most significant playwright of the new sentimental comedies, freely admitted the influence of Collier on his
writing of *The Lying Lover* (1703): 'Mr Collier had ... written against
the immorality of the stage. I was (as far as I durst for fear of witty
men, upon whom he had been too severe) a great admirer of his
work, and took it into my head to write a comedy in the severity he
required'.[12]

That Collier's attack was a rallying point rather than an instigation for reform in itself can be seen by turning to the first of
these new sentimental comedies, a play that was first produced at
the Theatre Royal, Drury Lane, in January 1696, two years before
the publication of the *Short View*. Its author was Colley Cibber – the
theatrical man-of-all-trades of his generation – and the play *Love's
Last Shift; Or, The Fool in Fashion*. Cibber was already well established
as an actor before he wrote this, the first of a succession of plays. In
writing it, it is apparent that he was intent on creating for himself a
role as Sir Novelty Fashion, the fool of the play's subtitle, 'a cox-
comb that loves to be the first in all foppery' as he is described in
the dramatis personae. And as such, he was undoubtedly successful, the playwright later claiming its continuing popularity over a
40-year period.[13] However, it is equally clear that Cibber had a very
strong sense of the changing theatrical climate and, although
audiences continued to enjoy the depiction of Sir Novelty, it was the
text of the plot that gave the play its main title that proved most
fitting to the immediate taste of the times.

Unsurprisingly, Cibber's play draws heavily from the by now
well settled machinery of the post-Restoration tradition; and in this
respect Sir Novelty is simply the latest in an already longish line of
satirised fop figures, descended most obviously from Etherege's Sir
Fopling Flutter, who also gives *The Man of Mode* its subtitle. The
initial plot lines seem little different from what has been on offer
previously, and the first-night audience would have taken some
considerable time to realise that they were in fact being lulled into a
false sense of expectancy.

Love's Last Shift, the first stage production of a man who continued to prove magnificently through his entire career that he
knew exactly when to bend with the wind, is evidence again of the
change in taste rather than a dangerous manifesto of opposition to
the contemporary theatrical canon. As he was to do throughout his
multifaceted theatrical career, Cibber reacted to what he correctly

understood was an audience demand. With this play, he offered them what was quickly heralded as the first of a new theatrical kind, the sentimental comedy, the prototype of which depended more than any of its successors on the Restoration comedy model it supposedly opposed.

Apart from his perpetuation of the tradition of the fop figure, there is the usual double plot – audience interest in narrative complexity by no means having lessened – each strand of which is concerned with the general themes of courtship and marriage. In the main plot the audience is introduced to Loveless, a man who has abandoned his faithful wife, Amanda, and pawned his estate 'to buy pleasure ... that is, old wine, young whores, and the conversation of brave fellows as mad as myself'. He has returned from foreign travel having exhausted his funds and in hope of replenishing them, 'for I hear my wife is dead: and to tell you the truth, 'twas the staleness of her love was the main cause of my going over'.

The audience scarcely needs the revelation, which it immediately receives, that his wife is not actually dead at all but hopes still for his return to her, to realise that there will be twists in this tale. Sir Novelty Fashion is not the only 'fool in fashion' in this play; and Loveless's assertion that his decision to abandon Amanda was based on the modern premise that no man of honour can continue to love his wife on the instalment of a new mistress gives further promise of a rather different conclusion to the plot than that anticipated by the husband. 'The joys of love are only great when they are new,' Loveless declares, with an unconscious irony, since he is unwittingly attempting the seduction of the disguised Amanda at the time, 'and to make them lasting, we must often change' (IV, ii).

This seduction, and its aftermath, provides the chief novelty of Cibber's play, as Loveless is tricked into an affair with a supposedly dead wife whom he fails to recognise (well, it has been ten years since he last saw her, she was only 15 when they married, and she has been not unattractively altered by smallpox!). She plays the reluctant mistress to him in a long scene, the eroticism of which is not in the least eroded by the fact that they are man and wife in the plot, a fact of only narrative interest to a voyeuristic audience; they retire off stage and to bed, before it is revealed to him that he has been 'robbing his own orchards', and that his enthusiastic bedfellow is in reality the still very alive Amanda playing the fallen woman in 'love's last shift'.

Amanda upbraids Loveless for the inhumane treatment of his wife and, already affected by the reasonableness of her attack, he is moved (as were the first-night audience) to tears as the faithful wife reveals the truth. Loveless repents: 'your words are uttered with such a powerful heart, they have awakened my soul, and strike my thoughts with horror and remorse'. His conscience awakened, Loveless ends the play with an absurdly improbable praise of married life and a diatribe against philandering, both of which run counter to all his earlier utterances in the play.

The theme is paralleled in reverse in the other main plot, in which the flirtatious Hillaria receives moral instruction and respectable happiness in marriage from the worthy older man, the Elder Worthy, whilst the younger, and equally worthy younger brother, Young Worthy – who has arranged the reconciliation between Amanda and Loveless – tricks the miserly Sir William Wisewould into parting with money and the hand of his rich daughter, Narcissa, a 'fortune' intended for the elder brother.

Now, there is evidently more than one way of considering what Cibber had to offer. With the exception of Sir Novelty Fashion, the characters in his play do not exist as those peculiar mixtures of celebration and satire that was usually the case in earlier Restoration comedies – in the figures of Dorimant in Etherege's *The Man of Mode* and of Horner in Wycherley's *The Country Wife*, to take two very different examples. The resolution of both plot strands depends upon a presentation of the characters as having gone through a process of education, and allows for their depiction at the end of the play as moral examples to be taken as desirable role models – and as moral examples in which the sentimental qualities of compassion and fidelity are united with those of common sense and reason, a definite move away from the earlier excesses of a Court-dominated world and towards the tighter confines of bourgeois conformity and respectability.

But equally, it is not difficult to observe, as many contemporaries did, that what Cibber was actually offering his audiences was three acts of conventional Restoration comedy intrigue, a fourth act of extreme sexual titillation, and a fifth act of moral reformation tacked somewhat awkwardly on to suit the changing tastes of the time. It is now a too easily held critical position to attack Cibber for the cynical about-turn of the main plot, and simply to re-rehearse this attack is to miss both the very strong virtues of the piece on stage and its historical significance. Cibber writes as a kind of juggler, attempting with incomplete success to create a harmony out of disparate and conflicting themes; the resultant confusion is there to be explored in production, and emphasises the way in which Cibber's play must be seen as a key turning-point in post-Restoration comedy precisely because it was written with an acute sense of the disparate and conflicting demands of a changing theatre audience.

There are a number of ways in which this sense of the novelty of Cibber's undertaking can be stressed, although in any account of the play's contemporary reception it must be acknowledged that without the continual interventions of Sir Novelty Fashion, a satirised figure drawn straightforwardly from the earlier comic tradition, the play would have appealed far less. However, it is notable that the main plot of the play is not concluded with the marriage of the two principal characters. If it is a form of remarriage that brings Amanda and Loveless back together, it is still the case that the predominating narrative interest of the play is focused on events after marriage. The willingness to consider life after the supposedly 'happy ending' is not in itself without precedent, and certainly there is more than one way of reading the move towards marriage of Dorimant and Harriet at the end of *The Man of Mode*, for instance; but it introduces a concern with the detailed workings of married life that is of vital importance in the work of both Vanbrugh and Farquhar, in particular, amongst the playwrights active around the turn of the century.

And whilst it is true that the other plot is concluded in traditional fashion with the marriage of the two brothers to their respective loves, the move towards marriage takes on a rather different resonance in ways which point to another key emphasis in Cibber's play. In the first act, after we have been introduced to Loveless, the park is left first for the Worthys to convey the burden of their complicated plot to marry the women of their choice, and then for the three women, Hillaria, Narcissa and Amanda 'in mourning', as if a widow. The two unmarried women are anxious to sound out Amanda on the merits of their intended husbands. Not surprisingly, Amanda declares herself an unsuitable referee – 'I am but an ill judge of men; the only one I thought myself secure of, most cruelly deceived me' – but is soon prevailed upon to offer her opinion. She is quite favourably disposed towards Hillaria's Elder Worthy, but finds her judgement of the younger brother coloured by memories of her own husband. Narcissa wants to know why she should 'not think of him':

> AMANDA: He puts me in mind of a man too like him, one that had beauty, wit, and falsehood.
> NARCISSA: You have hit some part of his character, I must confess, madam; but as to his truth, I'm sure he loves only me.
> AMANDA: I don't doubt but he tells you so, nay, and swears it too.
> NARCISSA: O Lord! madam, I hope I may without vanity believe him.
> AMANDA: But you will hardly, without magic, secure him.
> NARCISSA: I shall use no spells or charms, but this poor face, madam.
> AMANDA: And your fortune.
> NARCISSA: Senseless malice! [*Aside.*] I know he'd marry me without a groat.
> AMANDA: Then he's not the man I take him for.
> NARCISSA: Why pray – what do you take him for?
> AMANDA: A wild young fellow, that loves every thing he sees.
>
> (I, i)

Amanda's reminder to Narcissa that she comes with a fortune is a timely one; and, indeed, her future husband will end this first scene alone on stage accepting that Narcissa's waywardness does have its compensations – 'there's no fault in her £1000 a year, and that's the loadstone that attracts my heart'. And the doggerel verse with which he brings the act to a conclusion is straight from the heart of a younger brother:

> Women are changed from what they were of old:
> Therefore let lovers still this maxim hold,
> She's only worth, that brings her weight in gold.

Earlier, the Elder Worthy had considered his potential marriage in terms of his own more privileged financial position – 'I had need to have the best goods, when I offer so great a price as marriage for them' – and it is left to the younger brother to point out that Hillaria 'has beauty ... and money'.

Now, one of the things that distinguishes Cibber's play, and allows it to be labelled an 'exemplary' comedy, is that the older brother willingly supports the younger – something not found in *The Relapse* in the parallel plot – but this does nothing to detract from the way in which money, and its dominant importance in marriage arrangements, is foregrounded in the play. The carefree male libertines of the earlier comedies, possessed of inherited wealth, sometimes had more impoverished counterparts elsewhere in the plays, but the stress was always on the financially independent beaus. Increasingly, the emphasis was to turn to the supremacy of money as a motivating force in the new society.

In *Love's Last Shift* it is money, and not romance, that really turns the wheels of the plot. Narcissa's dismissal of the immoral Lady Mambre in Act II is made in revealing terms. 'She has been as great a hindrance to us virtuous women, as ever the Bank of England was to the city goldsmiths'. In Vanbrugh's *The Provoked Wife*, Constant echoes the theme when he declares that if the woman he loves will grant him her sexual favours he will perform a whole series of impossible tasks, the last of which will be to proclaim 'the Bank of England's grown honest' (III, i). The new Bank – along with the Stock Exchange, one of the necessary foundations for the development of capitalism – had been formed in 1694 as a way of dealing with the problem of state debts incurred in foreign wars. In part the jibes are directed at the allegations of corruption levelled at the new organisation – allegations that were scarcely surprising since the terms under which the Bank had been given its monopoly meant that, effectively, the whole of the country was literally owned by a few rich families – but they are, more generally, a reaction to the change in itself, seen, correctly, as a move away from the old landed interests of the courtly figures in earlier Restoration comedy and towards the appropriation of power by newer moneyed interests, as represented by figures who had been, at best, ignored in the earlier drama and more often satirised and reviled.

The distinction between an old world of virtue and a new one in which the financial machinations of the Bank serve as a metaphor of social change is picked up by Young Worthy with a knowing conjunction of images of the monetary advancement that may be achieved by resorting to marriage, and the venereal disease that may be contracted by resorting to prostitution: 'The reason of that is, madam, because you virtuous ladies pay no interest; I must confess the principal, our health, is a little securer with you'. And, of course, it is notable that Amanda's reconciliation with Loveless is effected not only by her playing the whore – to be bought and paid for – but because she is able to reveal that her uncle has recently died, leaving her £2000 a year, 'which I now cannot offer as a gift, because my duty, and your lawful right, makes you the undisputed master of it'. It is at this juncture that Loveless expresses himself absolutely happy; embracing his wife, he declares revealingly, 'I grasp more treasure, than in a day the posting sun can travel o'er'. At the beginning of the play we had quickly learned that Loveless had only returned to London because he was penniless, having mortgaged his estate in the pursuit of pleasure; and that the first favour accorded to both servant and master by Young Worthy is the gift of two guineas to 'provide us with a dinner and a brace of whores into the bargain'. In subsequent years the penniless beau was to become a frequent figure on the stage. But what is most significant about Cibber's treatment of the theme is the way in which it creates a link between the low-life and high-life characters, to give a picture of a society united in the pursuit of riches. Any sense that it is possible to separate the worlds of sex and marriage from those of commercial endeavour and financial betterment is shattered.

Indeed, although Loveless will end the play financially rescued and in the arms of his wife, his activities throughout most of the play are directed elsewhere. Loveless spends a great deal of the first three acts of the play announcing his intention of re-entering the sexual rounds of London, but it is significant that his projected liaisons are not with the society ladies, whose moves towards marriage and adultery chiefly preoccupy the earlier comedies. His is an entirely mercantile approach to sex, as a commodity to be bought and used. Young Worthy and Amanda cause him to stumble into his wife's bedroom. His energies are concentrated on the masks who must be bought, a past emphasis that Snap complains cost him the price of a pearl necklace for a single night with a 'Venetian strumpet', an outlay, the servant claims, that could have bought him 'the whole town over and over for half the price' back in London (I, i).

The connection between sex and money is paramount in Cibber's play, and the fact of money brings every strand of the plot to its final resolution. Just why this should be so is worth dwelling on a little, for it has implications for the drama that was to follow. In allowing for no formal separation between the essentially financial arrangements of both prostitution and marriage, *Love's Last Shift*

can be seen to be particularly aptly titled. Although a 'moral'
reading of the play will render a literal sense, it is also apparent that
love in the tradition of 'romance' really has come to its last shift.
Naturally, the marriages and settlements that conclude this and
later plays are embarked upon by spouses intent on protesting their
mutual love, but this is the happy coincidence that comes with the
necessary financial arrangements having been made.

Perhaps the most apt commentary on this connection comes
from within the play. Snap, having taken advantage of his master's
assignation with Amanda, drags her maid into the cellar for his own
sexual gratification. Discovered the following morning by the now
repentant Loveless, Snap reacts in horror to his suggestion that now
he has lain with the woman he must marry her, at least until the
terms are spelt out to him:

> LOVELESS: I'll give thee an hundred pounds with her, and thirty
>   pounds a year during life, to set you up in some honest
>   employment.
> SNAP: Ah, sir, now I understand you: heaven reward you. Well,
>   sir, I partly find that the genteel scenes of our lives are
>   pretty well over; and I thank heaven, that I have so much
>   grace left, that I can repent, when I have no more oppor-
>   tunities of being wicked. – Come, spouse, here's my hand,
>   the rest of my body shall be forth coming.

By 'genteel scenes' Snap refers to the world of prostitution and
licence outside marriage, but it is a hollow, ironic label, demonstrating as it does not a distinction of social worlds but an
interconnection in which the workings of a money economy are
everything. It is this emphasis that really distinguishes Cibber's play
from what had gone before, and not the 'sentimental' or
'exemplary' elements; and to realise this is to understand that
Vanbrugh's sequel to *Love's Last Shift*, interesting and innovatory
though it is in its own right, is actually a step back, an attempt to
recover an older world of Restoration comedy, an older world the
passing of which it is the chief merit of Cibber's play to chronicle.
That Vanbrugh should himself run into difficulties with that retro-
gressive move is also a measure of the process of change. The first
performed works of both dramatists are properly speaking 'problem
plays', attempting to solve dilemmas that the conventions of the

genre cannot readily cater for; what is most interesting is that they should have approached the problems from such different perspectives.

The fact that Cibber's play should centre on the problems of marriage rather, than as had previously normally been the case, the process of courtship leading to marriage, carries with it a further significance. In his autobiographical *Apology*, Cibber claimed that the reform movement resulted in a theatre in which 'indecencies were no longer wit, and by degrees the fair sex came again to fill the Boxes on the first day of a new Comedy, without fear of censure'.[14] Now, it would be absurd to attempt to construct a single female perspective on either the theatre of the time or on the attempts at reform. However, by the 1690s there is a clear sense of female members of the audience influencing the content of the comedies. This is not the place to pursue what is, in itself, a fascinating avenue of enquiry, but it is clear that, just as the very fact of female actresses playing female roles began to affect the presentation of women on the stage, the problematics of their relationships with men becoming increasingly a central theme of the plays, so the female members of the audience would be more likely to see the representation of their lives in realistic rather than idealistic terms as bringing a more direct relevance to their play-going. And for most of the 'respectable' female members of the audience, the problems attendant on marriage and its aftermath would have had a particularly strong resonance in a theatre whose ideology was still predominantly patriarchal.

After 1703 it became possible for 'ladies' to request revivals of plays. Of the 1091 performances of 180 different plays requested, the most popular was Cibber's *Love's Last Shift*, with 43 requested performances. This alone might demonstrate the power of the reform movement, but when we realise that the next most requested comedies – as opposed to tragedies, which were also requested frequently – were Farquhar's *The Constant Couple*, Steele's *The Tender Husband* and Vanbrugh and Cibber's *The Provoked Husband*, a distinct pattern begins to emerge.[15] For the wives in the audience the issue was marriage, and both Vanbrugh and Farquhar were to attempt to grapple with its problems in their most important plays.

4
Vanbrugh's *The Relapse* and *The Provoked Wife*

Vanbrugh's career as a writer for the theatre was not prolonged. His only completed original plays, *The Relapse* and *The Provoked Wife*, received their first performances in his first season (1696/7), and by 1707 he had contributed his final adapted piece, *The Cuckold in Conceit*, for the Queen's Theatre in the Haymarket, the theatre he had designed and had built, and the management of which had cost him dearly, both emotionally and financially. Unlike Farquhar, Vanbrugh does not appear to have regarded himself as a professional writer at all. He does not seem to have been particularly concerned either then or subsequently to become known as a playwright. His income derived largely from his work as an architect, and it was the fact of his financial involvement with the management of the new theatre in the Haymarket that he had designed that prompted the production of most of his later plays.

Whether or not he had begun on *The Provoked Wife* during his imprisonment in the Bastille, there seems little sense of urgency on Vanbrugh's part to write for the stage once he had returned to England. Indeed, it is characteristic of his elaborately casual attitude to the role of playwright that it should have taken a work by another writer to prompt him into action. There can be little doubt that for his first produced play Vanbrugh was prompted to provide a sequel to Cibber's *Love's Last Shift* by what he saw as the improbability of the ending. In his *Short Vindication* of 1698, he talks of the genesis of *The Relapse* as 'a pleasure to indulge a musing fancy, and suppose myself' in Loveless's place at the end of Cibber's play.[1]

In so musing, he is only too aware of the way in which Loveless's reformation must be considered in terms of the theatrical tradition that had given him life. He considers the character's situation: 'Loveless, He's so thoroughly weaned from the taste of his debauches, he has not a thought towards the stage where they used to be acted'.[2] And so it is that Loveless, brought back to London by Vanbrugh for business and not pleasure, is immediately led to the one place, the theatre, where he can be sure to see the implausibility of his reformation called into question. Ironically, when Loveless informs Amanda of the need to make the business trip, he talks of being 'dragged once more to that uneasy theatre of noise' that is the capital city (I, i). To reinforce the point, it is while attending the theatre that he first exchanges glances with the beautiful young widow who will help him to his 'relapse'. Vanbrugh emphasises the connection in his *Short Vindication*:

> The first place he tries his strength, is where he used to be the most sensible of his weakness. He could resist no woman before; He'll now show he can stand a Battalion of 'em; so to the Playhouse he goes, and with a smile of contempt looks coolly into the Boxes. But Berinthea is there to chastise his presumption.[3]

Vanbrugh's account is interesting, and should receive due consideration from any actor taking on the role of the relapsing Loveless, as should the degree of seriousness accorded the husband and wife's opening dialogue of mutual love and trust expressed by Simon Callow in his thoughts on playing the role.[4] It raises questions that take the play away from the straightforward mechanics of parody; although, clearly, the attempt to offer a psychological reading of Loveless's behaviour does owe much to the playwright's desire to offer a reply to Collier's charges.

It is worth considering this first visit to the playhouse in the context of the play. After the first scene between the husband and wife, two further ones in which the other plot is set in motion complete the opening act, and we do not see them again until Act II.

Loveless is trying to get Amanda to acknowledge that there are compensations attached to being back in town. She seems to find but one, that she is acting in accord with her husband's wishes. He cites, first, the 'conversation of the town' and then, carefully, adds, 'truly, with some small allowances, the plays, I think, may be esteemed another'. Amanda takes him up to make a point that would find sympathy with the reformers; but the reason for Loveless's carefully articulated list of qualifications gradually emerges, and it is clear that his thoughts are quite opposed to hers, however much his airing of them may be supposedly intended to exorcise them:

> AMANDA: The plays, I must confess, have some small charms, and would have more, would they restrain that loose obscene encouragement to vice, which shocks, if not the virtue of some women, at least the modesty of all.
>
> LOVELESS: But till that reformation can be made, I would not leave the wholesome corn for some intruding tares that grow amongst it. Doubtless, the moral of a well-wrought scene is of prevailing force. Last night there happened one that moved me strangely.
>
> (II, i)

Loveless's invocation of the 'innocent' rural image of corn and tares brings with it an ironic presage of things to come. The town, and the theatre, have reanimated his interest in matters of animal rather than vegetable husbandry. Amanda, naturally, presses to hear about it. Loveless says it will not bear repeating, and his wife insists until, inevitably, the story emerges. It is a story in which life and art, the past and the future, are inextricably linked, told to a wife to convince her that she has no need for jealousy!

> LOVELESS: Know then, I happened in the play to find my very character, only with the addition of a relapse; which struck me so, I put a sudden stop to a most harmless entertainment, which till then diverted me between the acts. 'Twas to admire the workmanship of nature in the face of a young lady that sat some distance from me, she was so exquisitely handsome.
>
> (II, i)

Loveless has been watching the very play in which he is performing, in the interludes of which he has been initiating the very thing that will lead to the connection being made good:

> LOVELESS: I did take heed; for observing in the play that he who seemed to represent me there was, by an accident like this, unwarily surprised into a net, in which he lay a poor entangled slave, I snatched my eyes away. They pleaded for leave to look again, but I grew resolute, and they obeyed.

Scarcely have the pair had time to discuss the significance of the matter when Berinthea is announced, 'a relation I have not seen these five years', says Amanda, innocently adding reported accounts of her beauty. She enters: 'Ha! By heavens, the very woman!', gasps Loveless, and from this moment the audience are left in no doubt that it is, indeed, *The Relapse* that is being performed for their entertainment.

Now, this sudden arrival strains dramatic credibility, and deliberately so. It is possible that Berinthea had taken the trouble to find out the name and married connection of her playhouse admirer, but Vanbrugh does not tell us this. It is a trick that he evidently enjoys for its comic potential, for he deploys it on two other occasions later in the play, when Syringe the Surgeon and Sir John Friendly prove to be at the very door of the house from which they have been urgently posted for. The effect in this instance, however, is to lay stress less on the farcical potential of the action than on the inevitability of Loveless's relapse. To re-echo his own words, he is 'surprised into a net', powerless to act against impulses which overwhelm him. It is left to an audience to reflect more coolly, if they are able, that this was the first temptation, the first woman to return an interested glance. The foundations of Loveless's reformation are proved to be pretty insubstantial. It is not just that he suffers a relapse, it is that the relapse is so immediate that is important, that underlines Vanbrugh's real objections to Cibber's about-turn.

And so matters proceed to the conclusion already witnessed on stage by Loveless. Berinthea is invited to lodge with them, and they are immediately visited by Worthy, 'a gentleman of the town', who, we quickly learn, is not only besotted with Amanda but is an ex-lover of Berinthea. The pair join forces against the married couple, the better to further their individual interests and, by Act IV, Loveless has crept secretly back into his own house and to Berinthea's chamber, where, after the shortest of verbal foreplay, he sets about the most comically unprotesting ravishment of the entire post-Restoration theatre:

> *Puts out the candles.*
> BERINTHEA: O Lord! are you mad? What shall I do for light?
> LOVELESS: You'll do as well without it.
> BERINTHEA: Why, one can't find a chair to sit down.
> LOVELESS: Come into the closet, madam, there's moonshine upon
>   the couch.
> BERINTHEA: Nay, never pull, for I will not go.
> LOVELESS: Then you must be carried.
> *Carrying her.*
> BERINTHEA *(very softly)*: Help, help. I'm ravished, ruined, undone.
>   O Lord, I shall never be able to bear it.
> [*Exeunt.*]

This is not the end of the play, or indeed of this strand of the plot; but before considering the problems that Vanbrugh encountered in concluding matters between Amanda and Loveless, it will be useful to consider the workings of the other plot that punctuates the narrative of the 'relapse'. For the playwright has other issues to take with *Love's Last Shift*. In a beautifully economical stroke Vanbrugh collapsed the action in Cibber's play concerned with the fop, Sir Novelty Fashion, and with the two Worthy brothers in pursuit of wives into a single secondary plot. The Elder Worthy does not appear in *The Relapse*, and the younger brother, still married to Narcissa, who neither appears nor is mentioned in the sequel, is subsumed into the main plot in pursuit of an adulterous affair with Amanda. The newly made up knight now becomes Lord Foppington, who acquires a younger brother, Young Fashion, as strapped for cash as was the Younger Worthy in *Love's Last Shift*, and at this juncture further divisions between the two plays become apparent.

Cibber's play was notable for the affable relations between the two brothers. Vanbrugh's depiction of the relationship between Lord Foppington and Young Fashion is more cynical, or more realistic we might say. There is no love lost between them and Foppington freely acknowledges that his brother would be as glad to hear of his death as he was to hear of that of the father whose estate then passed into the older man's hands. Indeed, he carefully avoids the possibility of the pair fighting a duel, declaring that whichever of them is killed will suit Young Fashion's purpose, to prosper or to perish.

Our introduction to Young Fashion (I, ii) comes in a scene in which, as so frequently in plays from this period, the economic plight of the younger brother in landed families is stressed. The impoverished master and his servant, Lory, are cheating the waterman out of his fee on their return to London from France, and contemplating in desperation the possibility of joining the army if Foppington will not lend him £1000.

The next scene takes us into the extravagances of Lord Foppington's dressing room, attended by tailor, sempstress, shoemaker, hosier, and periwig-maker. The Lord's altercation with the shoemaker is a borrowing from Molière's *Le Bourgeois Gentilhomme* of 1670[5] – and Vanbrugh's direct knowledge and use of the French drama, in a period that was anyway only too happy to borrow at will, is particularly important and of key significance in his later work – whilst his argument with the wig-maker over the size and weight of his wig draws directly from immediate memories of the comic deployment of two footmen and a sedan chair to carry on Cibber's enormous wig when playing Sir Novelty Fashion.[6]

To neither Young Fashion's nor the audience's surprise, Lord Foppington refuses resolutely to help his brother; and it is left to the old rogue, Coupler, to suggest a way of duping his brother and achieving financial security at a stroke. A marriage has been arranged, for money, between Lord Foppington and Miss Hoyden, the country-house-bound daughter of Sir Tunbelly Clumsey, a man as savagely caricatured as a member of the rural gentry as is Foppington as a representative of the urban aristocracy; this was something that rendered their eventual confrontation particularly striking for contemporary audiences, for whom the social distinctions would have seemed far more obvious, and far more important, than today.

In order to gain credence with the audience as a decent chap at heart, Young Fashion gives his brother one final chance to redeem himself and, rebuffed again, embraces the plan to impersonate

Foppington. Miss Hoyden proves to be one of the great parts for young actresses – a headstrong girl who is only too willing to marry Young Fashion in his assumed guise as Lord Foppington; willing, indeed, to take any man to whom she can be allowed access by the father who keeps her locked in her room. She is a supreme example of Vanbrugh's dictum of the urgency of the sexual itch – imprisoned against temptation, she is jealous that 'the young greyhound bitch can run loose about the house all day long'. She willingly accepts an immediate marriage and when, after Lord Foppington has arrived, and been trussed and imprisoned by her father, the truth is revealed, she happily embarks on a secret second marriage, having enjoyed a first taste of sexual pleasure and looking for further adventures in London. Coupler and Young Fashion are aided both in their initial plot and in the inevitable ultimate duping of Foppington by Miss Hoyden's nurse and a Parson Bull, who is so easily corruptible that his depiction alone was responsible for much of Collier's scorn for Vanbrugh's work. That the acquiescence of parson and nurse in confirming the fact of the first marriage – before Foppington has been able to find time to consummate the match – should occur because Young Fashion is able to promise the reverend a living of £500 per annum from his new estate (allowing the parson and nurse themselves to wed) is a part of the way in which the play insists on the connection between economics and human behaviour. Lord Foppington's extravagances, and his accompanying meanness, are the catalyst for a series of actions which unite town and country in a common interest against him.

That this is the case derives chiefly from the unusually prominent role that he plays in *The Relapse*. The foppish forerunners, and not only Sir Novelty Fashion, from which Vanbrugh draws so heavily had all been peripheral to the real action of the plays in which they appeared; their main function was to entertain, and to do so by their outrageously satirised nouveau riche behaviour, which was to be set against the 'model' of the polished beau of the old order – a Sir Fopling Flutter against a Dorimant in *The Man of Mode*, most obviously. Not only does Lord Foppington's access to all parts of the play allow virtually the only point of actual connection between the two plots – when he visits Loveless and Amanda in their town house, and is first slapped by the wife, then cut with a sword by the husband after he has attempted a public seduction of the woman – but he is a properly active protagonist in the entire play. The result is a more brilliantly rounded, albeit still satirised, fop than in any other post-Restoration play. The sincerity of Cibber's commitment to a morally reformed stage in *Love's Last Shift* was, incidentally, more than somewhat compromised by the fact that he willingly took on, and embellished, the part of Lord Foppington in Vanbrugh's sequel.

His visit to Amanda and Loveless in Act II, Scene i, for instance, is a piece of comic business without parallel. What is most remarkable about the fop that Vanbrugh has created is his absolute certainty. Having introduced himself, uninvited, into their house, he captures the conversation and proves utterly impervious to all attempts to put him down. His dialogue with the virtuous Amanda and the very unvirtuous Berinthea is wonderful in its depiction of a con-frontation of two completely different moral codes, and made the more enjoyable for an audience in that the more Foppington blunders into increasingly outrageous assertions to Amanda's mind, the more he thinks he is conquering her, not only by the external appearances of his dress and manner, on which he places so much importance, but by the force of his logic. So much so that, after a while, Amanda and Berinthea are forced to stop questioning his statements and to revert to the role of prompts for the further enjoyment of both themselves and the theatre audience. No longer needing to worry about the abstractions of the (to him) obvious truths of the lack of connection between books and reading and prayer and devotion, and having hijacked the entire social occasion, he is able to move on to his main topic of interest, himself. Even his library, full of unread books though it is, is lined with mirrors in which he can contemplate not only the exterior of his collection but of himself. Thinking, he declares, 'is to me the greatest fatigue in the world', at which Amanda asks him if he loves reading:

> FOPPINGTON: O, passionately, madam, but I never think of what I read.
> BERINTHEA: Why, can your lordship read without thinking?
> FOPPINGTON: O Lard! Can your ladyship pray without devotion, madam?
> AMANDA: Well, I must own I think books the best entertainment in the world.
> FOPPINGTON: I am so much of your ladyship's mind, madam, that I have a private gallery (where I walk sometimes) is

furnished [*sic*] with nothing but books and looking-glasses. Madam, I have gilded 'em, and ranged 'em, so prettily, before Gad, it is the most entertaining thing in the world to walk and look upon 'em.

AMANDA: Nay, I love a neat library too; but 'tis, I think, the inside of the book should recommend it most to us.

FOPPINGTON: That, I must confess, I am nat altogether so fand of. Far to mind the inside of a book is to entertain oneself with the forced product of another man's brain. Naw I think a man of quality and breeding may be much better diverted with the natural sprauts of his own. But to say the truth, madam, let a man love reading never so well, when once he comes to know this tawn, he finds so many better ways of passing the four-and-twenty-hours, that 'twere ten thousand pities he should consume his time in that. For example, madam, my life. My life, madam, is a perpetual stream of pleasure, that glides through such a variety of entertainment, I believe the wisest of our ancestors never had the least conception of any of 'em. I rise, madam, about ten a'clock. I don't rise sooner, because 'tis the worst thing for the complexion; nat that I pretend to be a beau, but a man must endeavour to look wholesome, lest he makes so nauseous a figure in the side-box, the ladies should be compelled to turn their eyes upon the play. So, at ten a'clack, I say, I rise. Naw if I find 'tis a good day, I resolve to take a turn in the park, and see the fine women; so huddle on my clothes, and get dressed by one. If it be nasty weather, I take a turn in the chocolate-house, where, as you walk, madam, you have the prettiest prospect in the world; you have looking-glasses all around you. But I'm afraid I tire the company.

BERINTHEA: Not at all. Pray go on.

Vanbrugh drew directly from Cibber's use of language in playing Sir Novelty for Lord Foppington's affectation of a superior drawl, and the printed text gives a good indication of the way in which the fop does become on stage that to which he aspires; despite his placement in the long line of stage stereotypes, he really is a one-off, an original, and the play's continuing popularity into the next century, long after the significance of Vanbrugh's play as a sequel had faded, owes more to his presence than anything else. For, in truth, *The Relapse* is a weakly constructed play. The two plots sit awkwardly alongside each other, and the farcical emphasis of the secondary plot, and even its intrusive presence, does much to detract from the residual seriousness of issues inherited by Vanbrugh in the Amanda/ Loveless plot. It was written very quickly, with the intention of being performed in the same season as *Love's Last Shift* in order to capital- ise upon its success. In the event it was not finished in time and had to await the next. It is riddled with easily correctable mistakes (Van- brugh, for no good reason, has it announced that Miss Hoyden is living with both her parents and then, unaccountably, and implaus- ibly, does not have the mother appear in the resultant chaos, for instance), but these are unimportant to the major problem which the play is quite unable to resolve – that of the conclusion of the main plot.

I argued earlier for a way of attempting to find a psychological reading of Loveless's, and by extension Amanda's, development in the play. In terms of the historical location of the play, this attempt is attendant with dangers, for Vanbrugh's audience were inevitably aware, and led by the play to retain this awareness, that what they were watching was, in a sense, *Love's Last Shift Part II*. This was true in a way that it was not subsequently, and particularly with the revival of interest in post-Restoration comedy in the latter part of this century. Today, *The Relapse* stands, and is produced, as a play on its own, and audiences need programme notes to learn that in important ways it does have a connection with Cibber's now almost unperformed prequel. It is thus more necessary, as well as more possible, for a production to examine questions of motivation outside of the play's original intention of parodying Cibber's 'senti- mentalism', especially if, as is apparent, Vanbrugh began to regard the play as something more than just a parody as he worked on it. And, indeed, modern rehearsal procedures are more inclined to pursue such directions.

However, whatever approach to the text is taken in performance, the problem of the play's conclusion remains. In using Cibber's play as a model, Vanbrugh perforce inherited many of the complexities with which the first play's characters struggled. The most important one concerns the way in which Vanbrugh wishes to call into ques- tion the absoluteness of Loveless's reformation, and the resultant effect on the presentation of Amanda as a dutiful wife. He has the couple open his play mouthing much the kind of affirmations of

fidelity that had closed *Love's Last Shift*. But his thesis throughout
the events that follow is that marriage cannot be defined in such
absolute terms in a real world. And so Loveless is tempted and falls.

But the force of Vanbrugh's attack, if attack it can be labelled, on
Cibber's presentation of the reformed husband rests on the need for
Amanda herself not to change, to remain faithful and chaste.
Otherwise, the significance of the 'relapse' is lost, and Loveless and
Amanda become just another post-Restoration comedy couple
going through the adulterous routine. That she should be so
resolutely courted by a man with the name of Worthy serves only to
highlight Amanda's very different, and moral, sense of worthiness
to that more worldly one understood by the town at large.

Consequently, in Act V, Scene iv, when Worthy finally is afforded
the opportunity of directly propositioning Amanda, the attempt
must be doomed to failure. We know that she is attracted to him,
and there is much in the scene that allows an actress scope to show
a woman caught between loyalty and sexual interest, especially
since she has been given firm proof of her husband's infidelity by
Berinthea. But she cannot give in, and so the scene is concluded
with Amanda extracting a promise from Worthy, that he may love
her only 'if, from this moment, you forbear to ask whatever is unfit
for me to grant'. It is, as she immediately adds, a problematic con-
cession: 'I doubt, on such hard terms, a woman's heart is scarcely
worth the having'.

After a last struggle, Amanda exits, leaving Worthy to a soliloquy
in which religious idealism and common sense are at war:

> Sure there's divinity about her; and she's dispensed some por-
> tion on't to me. For what but now was the wild flame of love or
> (to dissect that specious term) the vile, the gross desires of flesh
> and blood, is in a moment turned to adoration. The coarser
> appetite of nature's gone, and 'tis methinks the food of angels I
> require. How long this influence may last, heaven knows. But in
> this moment of purity, I could on my own terms accept her
> heart.

An actor would do well to ponder on the qualification offered by
that penultimate sentence. An angel Amanda may be, but we need
to remember just what Worthy's track record to date has been.
Vanbrugh has inherited him from *Love's Last Shift*, where his marriage

to Narcissa seemed more than in part prompted by the estate she would bring a penniless younger brother, and was accompanied by no sense that he would cease to play the field. Although, obviously, Vanbrugh is free to discard what he wishes of this Worthy's past – including Narcissa, who does not, and could not, ever appear – nothing we learn of him does much to alter the record. Though married to a woman, about whom he never talks, he has had Berinthea as a mistress and now courts another man's wife with the willing contrivance of that ex-mistress. Small wonder that Vanbrugh should leave affairs at that juncture. That is the last we hear from Amanda and Worthy, and Loveless has but one more sentence in the play. As Foppington mistakenly celebrates his marriage to Miss Hoyden in the final scene, he invites Loveless to take revenge on him for his attempt on his wife in the traditional manner, by cuckold-ing him. Loveless's reply, 'You need not fear, sir, I'm too fond of my own wife to have the least inclination to yours', is unfathomable. The stage directions tell us that Amanda, Worthy and Berinthea are also present at the feast as Loveless makes his final response. But it is hardly surprising that Vanbrugh does not have them speak. For, in the circumstances, what could they possibly say to each other? And how is Amanda meant to respond to her husband's words, if not sensibly placed to one side with Berinthea by a director and, in terms of stage conventions, out of ear shot? Certainly, there can be no question of allowing Amanda and Loveless to talk together. Vanbrugh's text prohibits it, and the inevitable lack of resolution hangs over the play's conclusion.

The audience is invited to forget the problems in the final flurry of the marriage feast and, after the revelations of Coupler's and Young Fashion's successful tricking of Foppington, it is left to the fop to conclude proceedings by not only having the last word but an epilogue which, in character, he devotes to talking about his own part in the play, totally excluding Amanda and Loveless from all mention. In order to achieve this quite massive evasion of a resolution, Vanbrugh perforce realises three quite extraordinary, and related, theatrical achievements. *The Relapse* is possibly the only acclaimed play in theatrical history to leave its main plot so definitively incomplete; it is probably the only one to allow the play's final scene to be entirely given over to the resolution of the secondary plot; and it is certainly the only one to do so in the unspeaking presence of all the characters from that main plot.

This uncertainty of resolution, and the accompanying problems with structuring the play, are also a feature of Vanbrugh's second, and last, completed original play, *The Provoked Wife*. He had written *The Relapse* for performance at the Drury Lane Theatre, which employed Cibber and had naturally performed Cibber's first play. *The Provoked Wife* was completed and first performed at Lincoln's Inn Fields by the rival company set up by Betterton. The move is, in itself, evidence of Vanbrugh's early entry into the theatrical politics that ensued after the setting up of a second London theatre company in 1695, thus ending the 13-year monopoly enjoyed by Drury Lane; and the haste with which the play was completed not only accounts for the weaknesses in its construction, but demonstrates Vanbrugh's sense of urgency in cashing in on the success of *The Relapse* for the benefit of the new company, after the mixed reception accorded his first 'adaptation', *Aesop*, at Drury Lane in the interim.

His new play again looked back to earlier drama, and a recent editor argues, indeed, that its general sense of indebtedness is such as to make the tracing of particular sources difficult, although he cites, in particular, Dryden's *Marriage à la Mode* (1672), Otway's *The Soldier's Fortune* (1681) and Etherege's *She Would if She Could* (1668).[7] And this is much as we might expect from a play that, although obviously finished after *The Relapse*, and owing much to a desire to develop some of the major themes of that play, was first embarked on much earlier.

In *The Provoked Wife* Vanbrugh again concentrates the interest on an unhappy marriage. Given that most plays in the earlier comedy tradition used the fact of marriage as the necessary resolution of the plot, the particular focus is significant. The three plays cited above can all be seen to offer precedents for this, but none considers with quite the same degree of seriousness as Vanbrugh the problems attendant on what is shown from the outset to be a totally misguided union. In addition, the fact that *The Provoked Wife* differs from virtually all the earlier plays in having nothing that can be properly defined as a secondary plot makes the emphasis stronger, drawing the activities of all the other characters into its plot resolution as it does.

That the husband in question should be a Sir John Brute gives a further indication of the novelty of Vanbrugh's intent. For, from the very opening words, we are left in no doubt that no attempt whatever will be made to engage our sympathies with the man. Sir

John starts the action alone on stage. His attack on marriage, both in general and in particular, is in stark contrast to Loveless's declaration of love and fidelity at the beginning of *The Relapse*, and sets him up as a stereotyped bully who will experience adultery as a victim rather than as a protagonist:

> SIR JOHN: What cloying meat is love – when matrimony's the sauce to it! Two year's marriage has debauched my five senses. Everything I see, everything I hear, everything I feel, and everything I taste – methinks has wife in't. No boy was ever so weary of his tutor, no girl of her bib, no nun of doing penance, nor old maid of being chaste, as I am of being married. Sure there's a secret curse entailed upon the very name of wife. My lady is a young lady, a witty lady, a virtuous lady – and yet I hate her. There is but one thing on earth I loathe beyond her; that's fighting. Would my courage come up but to a fourth part of my ill nature, I'd stand buff to her relations, and thrust her out of doors. But marriage has sunk me down to such an ebb of resolution, I dare not draw my sword, though even to get rid of my wife. But here she comes.
>
> (I, i)

And here, indeed, she does come, a Lady Brute whose opening question, 'Do you dine at home today, Sir John?', is parried by a husband who makes no attempt to disguise his loathing for her. In the dialogue that follows, Vanbrugh quickly generates sympathy for the 'provoked wife' in ways that suggest that, her husband's assertion of her 'virtuous' qualities notwithstanding, if she does eventually take her revenge lying down, then we will think none the worse of her for that. Left alone after his blunt abuse of her and her sex, she immediately reflects aloud on the possibility of obtaining a legal separation – 'these are good times; a woman may have a gallant, and a separate maintenance too' – or, much more problematic, a divorce. She attempts to welcome a new world of social contracts evidenced by the 1688 settlement that had brought William and Mary to the throne:

What opposes? My matrimonial vow? Why, what did I vow? I think I promised to be true to my husband. Well; and he promised to be kind to me. But he hasn't kept his word. Why then I'm absolved from mine. Ay, that seems clear to me. The argument's good between the king and the people, why not between the husband and the wife?

Lady Brute's invocation of the concept of marriage as a contract is already placed by her in a larger political context in which the notion of contract was central to the entire post-Restoration period, but in particular to the period after the Glorious Revolution of 1688. The introduction of the legal possibility of civil marriages during the Commonwealth period was but a first stage in the secularisation of the contract; but it is necessary to consider the particular implications of her connected argument, since it is more than an analogy. In her *Player's Scepters*, Staves quotes a contemporary judgement from Justice Hyde in respect of a wife's desertion of her husband:

> When the wife departs from her husband against his will, she forsakes and deserts his Government; erects and sets up a new jurisdiction; and assumes to govern herself, besides at least, if not against, the law of God and the law of the land. Therefore it is but just, that the law for this offence should put her in the same plight in the petit commonwealth of the household, that it puts the subjects for the like offence in the great commonwealth of the realm.[8]

The use of the term 'commonwealth' here brings a particular edge to the general principle enunciated, that a wife owes the same absolute allegiance to her husband as the subject does to the monarch. The wife's desertion is thus presented as akin to the action of the New Model Army *et al.* in separating from the monarch, and indeed having him executed. However, the notion of contract – which is of central import to all political debate of the later seventeenth and eighteenth centuries, as particularly exemplified in the work of Hobbes and Locke – was already implicit at the point of the Restoration. In 1688 it was established as a fundamental tenet of the agreement by which Parliament accepted William as monarch. So, Lady Brute's linkage of the two areas must be seen as a part of a larger questioning of the contractual nature of marriages – if the King has to debate terms, then so logically must the husband – and, more specifically, of the position of women in arranged and contractual marriages, a perfect example of which is that of the Brutes. It is, then, no accident that the position of married women, and in particular unhappily married women, should be foregrounded in the major plays of both Vanbrugh and Farquhar. So, before considering the development of the plot it is worth dwelling on the particular significance of the Brutes' marriage.

Whereas in *The Relapse*, Vanbrugh had to a large extent had the circumstances of Loveless's and Amanda's union foisted upon him by his appropriation of Cibber's account, here he is quite free to set up a marriage in any way that he wishes. We learn from the opening of Lady Brute's soliloquy that she had been warned of her future husband's likely conduct before she accepted the match – 'but I thought I had charms enough to govern him, and that where there was an estate, a woman must needs be happy; so my vanity has deceived me, and my ambition has made me uneasy'. In accepting Sir John, then, she had weighed the acquisition of an estate, with its consequent raising of her financial and social status, as a positive to be set against her knowledge of his bad qualities. That it was the sole determining reason for her acceptance has already been acknowledged by both parties in the opening dialogue:

> LADY BRUTE: What reason have I given you to use me as you do of
> late? It once was otherwise: you married me for love.
> SIR JOHN: And you me for money: so you have your reward, and
> I have mine.
>
> (I, i)

In the following act Sir John, bemoaning the fact of his marriage to Constant and Heartfree, is asked by them why, if he is not happy with 'one of the best wives in the world', he should have married her. His reply is blunt: 'I married because I had a mind to lie with her, and she would not let me'. And to Heartfree's 'why did you not ravish her?', he pleads the fear of recriminations from her relatives, and the fact that he then kept 'bad' company – 'fellows that went to church, said grace to their meat, and had not the least tincture of quality about 'em' (II, i).

This latter explanation of his refusal to play the role of courtly rake as a bachelor helps us to place Sir John in the panorama of post-Restoration society. He is not a member of the traditional landed gentry, whose interests and exploits were the chief object of celebration in earlier comedies. His lineage derives from the Commonwealth period, like that of Sir Nicholas Cully in Etherege's first play, *The Comical Revenge* (1664) – a man sneeringly described by the knight of the old order, Sir Frederick Frollick, a defiantly non-puritan beau, as having been made up by Cromwell 'for the transcendent knavery and disloyalty of his father'. Heartfree's question, and the nature of Sir John's response, creates an important distinction between the interests of these two worlds, and adds to the significance of Lady Brute's error in marrying for this particular estate.

Thus, although the particular ramifications of this marriage are now somewhat dimmed, Vanbrugh's audiences would have had a much more acute sense of the nature of this arranged union; and would readily be able to read into it not only an account of an individual misalliance, but issues of far greater social import. Sir John is to be viewed not only as a brute, but as an outsider, as a trespasser on the proper concerns of the traditional courtly rake, as represented most obviously by Heartfree. Viewed from the perspective of the earlier Court-dominated theatre, he can thus be seen to deserve all that befalls him, even before his particular nastiness is revealed. It is, after all, just what might be expected from such an upstart, and in this sense he stands in for the *nouveau riche* fop figure of the earlier comedies, a figure of key significance in Vanbrugh's first play and importantly missing from this.

We can take the general point further, however. Much has been made of the play's continual courting with the idea of divorce as a potential way out of the couple's dilemma. Lady Brute had introduced the idea at the outset and, in Act III, her husband also considers the possibility of proving her unfaithful, the only grounds then for divorce. The practical consequences of being forced to pay her a separate maintenance, as would have been the case at the time, are spelt out by Heartfree:

> SIR JOHN: If I could but catch her adulterating, I might be divorced from her by law.
>
> HEARTFREE: And so pay her a yearly pension, to be a distinguished cuckold.
>
> (III, i)

The plot set in motion by Vanbrugh is, then, concerned with much more than the dilemma of a particular couple. It raises questions that were crucial to the perpetuation of a changing order and to the family politics of arranged marriages; and it offers to do so in ways that highlight the particular dilemma of the women who were effectively sold off in order to facilitate the workings of such arrangements. No previous playwright had taken the debate so far and, although Vanbrugh's account of the problems never approaches the tragic as the novelist Samuel Richardson was to do in *Clarissa* (1747–8), *The Provoked Wife* must be seen as a key document in the history of that debate.

Freedom from the legal shackles of marriage cannot, then, be presented as a way out for Lady Brute – and a role as tragic heroine seems always unlikely. But she is no Amanda and when her husband leaves the stage in the first scene, she is quick to make this distinction clear to the audience once she is joined by her niece:

> LADY BRUTE: In short, Belinda, he has used me so barbarously of late, that I could almost resolve to play the downright wife – and cuckold him.
> BELINDA: That would be downright indeed.
> LADY BRUTE: Why, after all there's more to be said for't than you'd imagine, child. I know according to the strict statute law of religion I should do wrong; but if there were a Court of Chancery in heaven, I'm sure I should cast him.
> BELINDA: If there were a House of Lords you might.
> LADY BRUTE: In either case I should infallibly carry my cause.
>
> (I, i)

Her conjuring with the activities of the Court of Chancery, which could not provide the required remedy, and the House of Lords, through which the first private bill was to pass granting the first such divorce in 1698, highlights the impossibility of such a salvation from her misery.[9] She has already established the terms on which she might find both revenge on her husband and personal happiness with the suggestion of adultery. It is a suggestion that, with its attendant course of action, will keep Lady Brute firmly within the conventions of post-Restoration comedy, albeit unusually from a proto-feminist perspective.

Belinda supports her aunt against the husband and has a practical suggestion to make. The general idea accepted, she offers a particular man, Constant, 'one that thinks you hate him, as much as I know you love him'. The wife is soon brought to admit both her knowledge of Constant's admiration of her and hers of him, and readily develops Belinda's introduction of the imagery of siege warfare and conquest more conventionally associated with the language of male characters in the comedies:

> BELINDA: 'Tis well Constant don't know the weakness of the fortifications; for o' my conscience he'd soon come on to the assault.
> LADY BRUTE: Ay, and I'm afraid carry the town too. But whatever you may have observed, I have dissembled so well as to keep him ignorant. So you see I'm no coquette, Belinda.... After all, 'tis a vicious practice in us to give the least encouragement but where we design to come to a conclusion. For 'tis an unreasonable thing to engage a man in a disease which we beforehand resolve we never will apply a cure to.
>
> (I, i)

The appropriation of the masculine imagery of sexual conquest is important. Given the placement of this dialogue before we have our first sighting of Constant and long before he and Lady Brute are finally allowed alone on stage together, it has the effect of positing a move for the character away from a traditionally passive and feminine stage role, in favour of the active mode associated with the male libertines, again here well represented by Constant's friend Heartfree. Although, Lady Brute is anything but a libertine. She has not been willing to play the flirt; and when she finally makes an offer, it will be after due consideration of the consequences and in earnest.

Her relationship with Belinda, presented throughout the play as a resolutely independent young lady intent on determining her own choice of partner free of the kind of restraints that have led Lady Brute to her present quandary, further strengthens this sense of a specifically feminist slant to the play's argument; although, of course, to use such a description about the play is historically and ideologically problematic. However, the degree of frankness in the pair's discussion about men and sex in Act III, Scene iii (whilst preparing for bed) is quite remarkable for its time.

Vanbrugh concludes his opening scene with Lady Brute and Belinda agreeing 'how wrong men's maxims are' and expressing a belief that 'we should outdo 'em in the business of the state too'. Naturally, they will be given no opportunity to prove their superiority in the 'intrigues of government', and the final words of the scene are given to a Lady Brute already clearly with her future in mind: 'we have intrigues of our own that make us more sport, child'. And then, before we meet any of the other male characters, we move to the dressing room of Lady Fancyful, a woman whose vanity has been bitterly attacked by Lady Brute and Belinda in the first scene – 'She concludes all men her captives; and whatever course they take, it serves to confirm her in that opinion'.

With Lady Fancyful we approach as near as the play gets to a subplot. Although her actions are all entangled in the main events surrounding the Brutes, she is the female equivalent of the traditional fop figure. All affectation, she speaks French with her maid, Mademoiselle – though at least Vanbrugh is capable of giving the pair correct French with which to address each other; she is the embodiment of a femininity that is absolutely at odds with that of the other two women, and her introduction at this point serves to emphasise the point of the distinction. Believing herself sexually in control of virtually the entire male population of polite society, she ends the play caught out in a ridiculous attempt to disrupt the relationships of the other main characters and still alone.

That she should be first seen at her prolonged morning toilette is inevitable and telling; it places her in exactly the same position at the outset as Lord Foppington, for instance. In the middle of her preparations, through which the constantly rewarded maid offers a continuously flattering commentary, she is interrupted first by the arrival of a new song, which she has to hear performed, and then by a letter. It is not quite the billet-doux that she is expecting. The letter is an invitation; if 'you have a mind to hear of your faults, instead of being praised for your virtues, take the pains to walk in the Green Walk in St James's Park with your woman an hour hence'.

The second act opens with the two women meeting with the letter writer, Heartfree, who gives her an unwanted lecture on the absurdity of her affectation. The women sweep off, but a scene later we are back in Lady Fancyful's house where we learn, unsurprisingly, that 'this Heartfree has bewitched me', an admission that leads to the decision to invite him to a further assignation.

In the meantime, Heartfree has met up with his friend Constant in the park. Their dialogue, briefly interspersed, after his arrival, by Sir John's diatribe against his wife and marriage in general, is concerned with Constant's profession of the impossibility of his love for Lady Brute, and with his friend's attempts to persuade him out of serious emotional entanglements. In the argument that ensues, both men live up to the promise of their names. Heartfree tells him that the difference between them is that, 'I persuade a woman she's an angel, she persuades you she's one' – and thus sexually unavailable. He then offers his recipe against falling in love. Given his attempt to persuade Lady Fancyful of the pointlessness of her superficial charms and affectations, it is of particular thematic significance.

Heartfree tells Constant that he is unimpressed by the exterior of women, by the things that are more justly the due of her tailor, her shoemaker, and so on: 'I consider her as pure nature has contrived her, and that more strictly than I should have done our old grandmother Eve, had I seen her naked in the garden'. The imagery of Eden, with its attendant and opposing associations of woman as temptress and man as devil, is found frequently in post-Restoration comedies – forming a strong series of links in *The Man of Mode*, for example – and Vanbrugh makes much use of it in this play. Its effect is to suggest a duality of responsibility, in which each sex is able to blame the other by reference to versions of the same mythology.

But Heartfree is intent on appropriating it for quite a different purpose. His concern is to look beyond the surface appearance of women, and to see into their hearts, where he has found only 'pride, vanity, covetousness, indiscretion, but above all things, malice'. These conclusions thus justify his professed role as a rake and a libertine, with a hearty disinclination to settle for the shackles of matrimony. His strategy for survival when faced with a beautiful woman is revealingly simple and, it might be noted in passing, simply revealing:

> HEARTFREE: Then for her outside, I consider it merely as an
> outside; she has a thin tiffany covering over just such stuff
> as you and I are made of. As for her motion, her mien, her
> airs, and all those tricks, I know they affect you mightily. If
> you should see your mistress at a coronation, dragging her

peacock's train, with all her state and insolence about her, 'twould strike you with all the awful thoughts that heaven itself could pretend to from you; whereas I turn the whole matter into a jest, and suppose her strutting in the selfsame stately manner, with nothing on but her stays and her under scanty quilted petticoat.

(II, i)

Now, whilst it is easy to see that the general drift of Heartfree's critique applies easily enough to Lady Fancyful, he will have to learn that not all women are the same. And, as he becomes entangled in Constant's attempts to win over the aunt, he rapidly finds himself helplessly in love with the niece. When Sir John later finds Constant and Heartfree in his closet, the former interrupted in his liaison with Lady Brute, a plan is concocted for Belinda and Heartfree to marry; and despite Lady Fancyful's vain attempts to reveal all, the pair close the play heading for the church with just this intention.

Heartfree has learned that all his rationalisations are helpless when confronted with real passion – as Constant stresses to him by asking about his views on his love's quilted petticoat – but it is Belinda's decision to marry her estate to his lack of one that carries the real burden of interest for the audience. As she had always given promise of doing, she considers her actions coolly before agreeing to marry a man without money, accepting a slight lowering of her living standards as a reasonable penalty for not making the same mistake as her aunt. But she is no sentimental heroine: reminded by her aunt that Heartfree is 'but a younger brother, and has nothing', she carefully measures love against common sense:

> BELINDA: 'Tis true; but I like him, and have fortune enough to keep above extremity. I can't say I would live with him in a cell upon bread and butter. But I had rather have the man I love, and a middle state of life, than that gentleman in the chair there, and twice your ladyship's splendour.

(V, ii)

Once again Vanbrugh has swerved attention away from the chief preoccupation of the plot at the outset, the unhappy marriage of the

Brutes, in favour of the traditional marriage resolution. Zimansky sees this refusal to provide a happy ending to Lady Brute's dilemma as a virtue of the play. 'The central problem, the incompatible marriage, can be shown and can be discussed, but it cannot be resolved: Sir John and Lady Brute are in the same situation at the end of the play as at the beginning.'[10] However, to argue that the lack of the desired divorce represents a lack of resolution is to miss the point of the distinction between the presentation of Sir John as an undeveloping character and Lady Brute as one who undoubtedly has changed and hardened in her resolve to live her own life in future.

Much of the audience enjoyment of the play comes from Sir John's drunken cavortings about the stage; dragging himself from the tavern to create mayhem on the town, he steals a clergyman's gown from a 'dissenting journeyman tailor' – fair game as far as most of the audience would have been concerned – disguises himself as a reverend, is arrested, released and blunders briefly into an assignation in Spring Garden between the disguised Lady Brute and Belinda with Constant and Heartfree. But this farcical comedy does nothing to endear him as a character. Believing himself already cuckolded by the end of the play, and too cowardly to have the matter out with Constant, we are left in no doubt that he shortly will be, and that Lady Brute will find occasions to make her married life more pleasant – even if the audience are not to be shown it. Any production of the play would do well to consider where exactly Constant and Lady Brute are placed in relation to each other and just what they are about as the Belinda/Heartfree plot is brought to its pre-married resolution.

The Epilogue is given over to the actresses playing Lady Brute and Belinda; and, although they speak as actresses, it is hard not to make a connection between their final references to the negotiations currently taking place for the male-organised Treaty of Ryswick, and their earlier stated intent of taking a properly feminine interest in any governing that needs doing:

> LADY BRUTE: But at grand treaties hope not to be trusted
>   Before preliminaries are adjusted.
> BELINDA: You know the time, and we appoint the place,
>   Where, if you please, we'll meet and sign the peace.

5
Vanbrugh's *The Confederacy* and Other Adaptations

Although Vanbrugh is now generally thought of as the writer of just two plays, *The Relapse* and *The Provoked Wife*, an exclusive concentration on these two works gives a completely misleading sense of his place in his contemporary theatre. In addition to the incomplete *Journey to London*, he was responsible (or, in the case of *Squire Trelooby*, partly responsible) for nine other plays. To ignore them is to misunderstand the nature of his achievement and, also, the particular role that he saw for himself as a theatrical practitioner.

That they are now effectively forgotten pieces is a result largely of the fact that they are all, some more loosely than others, adaptations of pre-existing and, with one exception, non-British plays. In a period in which the assimilation of material from French drama, and in particular that of Molière, was of major importance, Vanbrugh stands alone. He more than any of his contemporaries was responsible for introducing direct versions of French drama to the London stage. Indeed, his very first effort for the Queen's Theatre, the building and management of which were to cost him so dearly, was an adaptation of Dancourt's *Les Bourgeoisies à la Mode*, a play first performed in Paris in November 1692, the very month that Vanbrugh was released from the Bastille, and almost certainly attended by him.

Vanbrugh's adaptation, *The Confederacy* (1705), had been preceded by his collaborative adaptation of Molière's *Monsieur de
Pourceaugnac*, *Squire Trelooby*, which played at Lincoln's Inn Fields in
1704 (and was revived at the Haymarket in 1706); and it was
followed by his versions of two more of Molière's plays, *Le Depit
Amoreux* (*The Mistake*, 1705), and *Le Colc Imaginaire* (*The Cuckold in
Conceit*, 1707). Vanbrugh never wrote an original play for his own
theatre, a fact which should alone call for a rethinking about the
particular nature of his contribution to the contemporary stage. For
these adaptations were always more than simply attempts at direct
translation, and the playwright brought to even the weakest of
them a degree of characteristic wit. Thaler says, 'Vanbrugh was
never a slavish borrower and even his rather indifferent efforts are
usually redeemed from utter futility by raciness of language and
occasional strokes of vigorous caricature'.[1]

His awareness of the significance of his endeavours can be seen
quite early, in the published Preface to the first of these adaptations,
Aesop (1696). Vanbrugh talks of the mixed reception with which
Boursault's *Les Fables d'Aesope* had been met after its first performance in Paris on 10 January 1690. It was several nights before it
was accepted, although it eventually lasted for 43 performances. It
is highly likely that Vanbrugh saw the play when he was in Paris,
and certainly he brings to all his adaptations a sense of familiarity
with the originals which is quite unusual at this time. He apologises
for his deviations from the original, alterations which he evidently
made with a view to gaining acceptance for it at Drury Lane:
'Though, after all, had I been so complaisant to have waited on his
Play word for word, 'tis possible even that might not have ensured
the success of it. For though it swam in France, it might have sunk
in England. Their country abounds in cork, ours in lead.'[2]

He speaks almost as an ambassador, and it is possibly more
appropriate to think of him as a man consciously intent on introducing examples of the foreign drama to the English stage, than
as a lazy freebooter of others' works. However, he is not consistent
in his acknowledgement of source material; and whereas with *Aesop*
he is eager to present the work as an adaptation, by the time of *The
Confederacy*, an audience listening to the Prologue is led to believe
that what they are about to see is 'a new play' written by a man by
now much preoccupied with 'building houses here to oblige the
peers'.[3]

That aside, it is difficult to make much of a case on the basis of *Aesop*, which, with its short sequel *Aesop, Part II*, was performed at Drury Lane in the 1696/7 season, shortly after the successful introduction of *The Relapse*. Despite the presence of Cibber in the title part and Pinktheman trading on his popularity with a succession of cameo roles, it was too obviously a slight piece. A basic plot, in which the overbearing Governor of Syzicus seeks to gain status and influence by attempting to force his beautiful young daughter to marry the influential old Aesop, is concluded by Aesop realising the absurdity of his ambitions and arranging her union with the young man she truly loves. It is a skimpy narrative and its progress serves the purpose largely of affording Aesop the opportunity of demonstrating the absurdities of other characters' ambitions by means of a series of familiar fables, that he may eventually realise the folly of his own.

In a play that conjures with questions of political rule – and borrows directly from Menenius's parable of the belly from Shakespeare's *Coriolanus* to do so – the over-riding theme is a plea for the status quo, however poorly the various representatives of government may be seen to be performing. For instance, in *Aesop, Part II*, Vanbrugh introduces a country gentleman into the scene, intent on gaining Aesop's support in his endeavour to have himself and his family take over the running of the state and its army, on the basis that they would do a far better job. Aesop concludes a longish question and answer session with a, by now, predictable demonstration of the absurdity of the man's logic:

AESOP: But, Sir, when I have done you this mighty piece of service, I shall have a small request to beg of you … in behalf of the two Officers who are to be displaced, to make room for you and your son.

GENTLEMAN: The Secretary and the General?

AESOP: The same. 'Tis pity they should be quite out of business; I must therefore desire you'll let me recommend one of 'em to you for your Bailiff, and the other for your Huntsman.

GENTLEMAN: My Bailiff and my Huntsman? – Sir, that's not to be granted.… Because one would ruin my land, and the other would spoil my fox-hounds.… Why Sir, do you think that men bred up for the State, and the Army, can understand the business of ploughing and hunting.

AESOP: I did not know but they might.

GENTLEMAN: How could you think so?

AESOP: Because I see men bred up to ploughing and hunting, understand the business of the State and the Army.

GENTLEMAN: I'm shot – I haven't one word to say for myself – I never was so caught in my life.

All in all, Vanbrugh did well to wonder in his Prologue about the reception of a piece so foreign in its interests to the London theatre:

> Barren of all the graces of the stage,
> Barren of all that entertains this age.
> No hero, no romance, no plot, no show,
> No rape, no bawdy, no intrigue, no beau:
> There's nothing in it, with which we use to please ye:
> With down right dull instruction, we are to tease ye.

Despite his own reservations, it was this piece, together with *Love's Last Shift* and *The Relapse*, that allowed the Drury Lane Theatre to survive against all the hopes of the new Lincoln's Inn Fields company that it might collapse. And it was followed the next season by his version of Dancourt's *La Maison de Campagne* (of 1688, and again probably seen by Vanbrugh during his time in Paris). *The Country House* (1698) proved, indeed, to be the only lasting success of that season,[4] and was revived as a part of the increasingly popular double bill through to the second half of the eighteenth century.

Vanbrugh's adaptation works well. Even though he expanded the original one act to two, the sheer profusion of characters on which the plot depends both for its point and its humour, and the necessary squashing of the action into a short amount of stage (and real) time, move the comedy away from that of wit and manners towards farce. There is the traditional young man in pursuit of a young lady, a marriage plan prohibited by an irascible father, but there is no room on this crowded stage to take their dilemma particularly seriously. The father, the miserly lawyer, Mr Barnard, has purchased the country house in which the action is set by, we learn, 'ruining honest people in town'. And his is the real dilemma of the play. Threatened with financial ruin from the upkeep of the estate, and married to a woman who does not know how much she squanders because 'I don't understand Arithmetic', he is besieged by a succession of uninvited guests who threaten to complete the process. His solution, to turn his house into the most expensive inn in the neighbourhood, and thus be rid of all the free-loaders, brings matters to a resolution, especially when his daughter's suitor gets Mr Barnard's consent to their marriage in exchange for keeping quiet about the King's deer his cook has shot to provide for his guests.

There is much hustling and bustling in and out of doors and closets, and the predominant feeling is that nothing is to be taken seriously. Given Vanbrugh's undoubted talent for converting the rather more courtly language of Dancourt into a more appropriately rural boisterousness of tone – although, jokingly, he makes a point of retaining the French location of the play – it is not surprising that it should have succeeded.

Vanbrugh's next adaptation, *The Pilgrim* (first performed at Drury Lane in 1700), also contained the familiar plot motif of a tyrannical father. Alphonso is intent on marrying his daughter, Alinda, to Roderigo when she is in love with, and loved by, his deadly rival, Pedro. Again the play is concluded in traditional manner with the celebration of the union of Alinda and Pedro. But it is otherwise quite unlike anything else Vanbrugh ever attempted, and is certainly his least satisfactory work as a result.

The Pilgrim was his version of Fletcher's earlier play of the same name. A few characters have been added, but the chief difference is that Vanbrugh abandoned the blank verse of the original in favour of a colloquial prose idiom more to the taste of his contemporaries. The result is an absurdly anachronistic plot, involving all the melodramatic paraphernalia of disguise, pursuits, scenes in a madhouse, and gangs of outlaws and roving pilgrims of the original. The transposition of all the romantic matter of a play, which clearly had some relevance when it was first acted at Court in 1621, on to the public stage in 1700 renders the whole thing quite ridiculous. By 1700, the briefly attempted revival of heroic, blank-verse dramas and tragedies of the immediate post-Restoration period was all but over, its essentially courtly connotations at odds with the interests of the changing audiences. And, although the original is a romance rather than a tragedy, it has echoes not only of Shakespeare's *Two Gentlemen of Verona*, with its deployment of pursuit, disguise and outlaws, but also of his *King Lear*, with its narrative use of madness and the introduction of a fool. If it was a pretty worn-out piece of mechanics by 1621, by 1700 it carried batteries whose energy had long since leaked away.

Cibber chose wisely. Offered any part he wanted, he opted for the minor cameos of the freshly introduced stuttering cook and the mad Englishman in the asylum: 'In which homely characters I saw more matter for delight, than those that might have had a better pretence to the amiable'.[5] In addition, he was given both the Prologue and the Epilogue to speak.

The original was perhaps most notable for the way in which the two main female characters, Alinda and her faithful maid Juletta, were carried around the countryside in a series of largely male disguises in a manner entirely characteristic of a theatre still dependent on male actors to play the roles. And much play is made of the fact that no one ever recognises these two 'boys' until they are off stage. But it is a joke that has worn very thin by the time it has gone through Vanbrugh's hands, and into the possession of women to play the roles. Apart from Cibber's contributions, its only real dramatic interest for contemporary audiences came from the fact that Mrs Oldfield – the actress first discovered by George Farquhar – was allowed full rein to display her talents in the many disguised roles of Alinda, only her second major part on the stage. Although it was revived, both at Drury Lane and at the new Queen's Theatre, as well as putting in occasional appearances through best part of the eighteenth century, it then found the oblivion that it deserved. And Vanbrugh never again repeated the experiment of raiding the earlier English drama.

Considered from a modern perspective it has all the signs of a desperation to find something, almost anything, with which to prop up the ailing fortunes of the theatre. Indeed, the major point of the entire exercise appears to have been to offer the elderly Dryden some means of financial support in exchange for giving his name to the adaptation, and thus a sorely needed boost to the Drury Lane company, by the provision of the Prologue, Epilogue and Masque with which the play is concluded.

The Secular Masque is the most curious feature of the play. In terms of the play's narrative it serves to celebrate the reformation of Roderigo, won over by the combined virtue of Alinda and Pedro (who has spent much of the play disguised as a pilgrim), and the latter's marriage, grumpily accepted by an Alphonso who has earlier suffered incarceration in the asylum in pursuit of his daughter. But it is really a tribute to the dawning of the new century, with the marriage taking place on what we learn is the King's birthday. So, the elderly Dryden is able to look back over the political events of his earlier life in a way that is often at odds with the concerns of the current Protestant reign of Queen Anne. Thus, 'Diana represents the reign of James I, with whom hunting was a passion, and happy vinous evenings a relaxation. Mars stands for the Civil Wars and Venus for the courtly debaucheries of the early Restoration'.[6]

This allegorical conclusion was certainly apposite for a Dryden who was now an avowed Catholic, but looks more than a little problematic in a Vanbrugh play, and it is as well that the allegory was not too transparent. Perhaps there was a conscious decision to revive a play that was in the theatrical repertoire around the time of the poet's birth as some kind of tribute. If this was so, it was particularly appropriate. The play's Prologue and Epilogue allowed the poet his final statements on the state of literary affairs.[7] It was first performed in April 1700. On 1 May, Dryden died, aged 69, and the printed text refers sadly to him as 'the late great poet'.

Vanbrugh's next offering for the Drury Lane Theatre, *The False Friend* of 1702, was to be his last. Thereafter, his efforts would be confined to his support for the new company at the Queen's Theatre in the Haymarket. *The False Friend* is based on Le Sage's *Le Traitre Puni* of 1700, a play which was in its turn a version of a Spanish verse drama, *La Traicon Busca el Castigio* by Francisco de Rojas Zorilla. Yet again, its central plot is concerned with the anguish of a daughter, Leonora, who is in love, and is loved by Don Guzman, but whose tyrannical father, Don Felix, has betrothed her, sight unseen, to another, Don Pedro.

The plot is further complicated by the presence of a third man, Don John, for whom marriage forms no part of his plans for the unfortunate lady. Warned off his pursuit by Don Guzman early in the play, Don John is the more keen for the conquest, as he explains to his servant, Lopez:

> DON JOHN: I thought at first the coxcomb came upon another subject which would have embarrassed me much more.... I was afraid he came to forbid me seeing his sister Isabella, with whom I'm on very good terms.

LOPEZ: Why now that's a hard case, when you have got a man's sister, you can't leave him his mistress.

DON JOHN: No changeling, I hate him enough, to love every woman that belongs to him; and the fool has so provoked me by his threatening, that I believe I shall have a stroke at his mother, before I think my self even with him.

LOPEZ: A most admirable way to make up accounts truly.

DON JOHN: A Son of a Whore! s'death, I did not care sixpence for the slut before, but now I'll have her maidenhead in a week; for fear the rogue should marry her in ten days.

(I, i)

The immediate entrance of the father, wondering that Don John's attentions towards his daughter are not accompanied by an offer of marriage, only serves to fuel his desire for libidinous gratification rather than the legal contract; and, having seen off the father with a reiterated sense of affront that he might wish to marry his daughter, he again stresses the mechanical nature of his intent, in the familiar imagery of warfare: 'I am going, Lopez, to double my attacks: I'll beat up her quarters six times a night, I am now downright in love; the difficulties pique me to the attempt, and I'll conquer or I'll die'.

Interestingly, one of the changes made by Vanbrugh from his source is to swap the characters of Don Pedro and Don John, so that the latter brings with his name all the traditional associations of the 'Don Juan' figure. And certainly, Don John proceeds to so interpret his role, lying, cheating and unsuccessfully attempting to rape Leonora under the guise of darkness.

Foiled in his attempt by the timely arrival of Don Guzman – still in love with Leonora even after she has been through an as yet unconsummated marriage ceremony with Don Pedro – the would-be rapist is able temporarily to turn the matter to his advantage, accusing her rescuer of the attempt. And so the play creaks melodramatically on, culminating in the death of Don John, unwittingly stabbed in the darkness by his friend, Don Guzman, having been enjoined by him to protect his wife's honour in an absence to visit his dying father. The false friend dies, and Leonora is reconciled to a life with the man chosen for her by her father. The last words in the play are addressed by her to Don Pedro:

You to yourself alone, shall owe your smart,
For where I've given my hand, I'll give my heart.

In one sense, Vanbrugh has done what he promised he would in the play's Prologue, where he addresses directly 'You dread reformers of an impious age', promising Collier and co. a piece that will satisfy their desires for correct models of behaviour. The villainous rake is killed off and the play concluded with an affirmation of daughterly duty and respect for the marriage vows. Vanbrugh's Prologue is explicit with regard to the issues involved:

To gain your favour, we your rules obey,
And treat you with a moral piece today;
So moral, we're afraid 'twill damn the play.

However, the schematic account of the plot offered by me disguises the very real problems encountered by any attempt to engage critically with the play. For, in all the ways that might allow for the construction of a 'moral' reading of events, the play is deficient: the characters are wooden and implausible – with the obvious exception of Don John and his comically conceived servant, one of the many rogue servants deployed by Vanbrugh, showing a particular indebtedness to their use in French comedy, 'ultimately descended from the Roman crafty slave';[8] the action over-reliant on the absurdly contrived machinery of melodrama; and, most importantly, the conclusion, in which Leonora is supposedly reconciled to her lot, totally unprepared for and equally unconvincing.

The attendant problems are so great that, were the piece more substantial in its scope, it would be possible to suggest a rather more subversive reading of the 'moral' conclusion – to note that the daughter is forced into marriage against her wishes, and to observe that if this is an attempt to provide a properly correct ending, then so much the worse for moral propriety. For the play pulls in two opposing directions: that represented by the libidinous desires of a Don John whose expressed programme looks back to the excesses of earlier Restoration comedy; and that represented by the provision of a narrative closure that confirms the sanctity of marriage and the family in a new world of contractual responsibilities. The two simply do not fit together, and that they do not was probably in large part responsible for the play's indifferent reception. But that they do not fit within the structure of the play did receive a final comment in performance. Vanbrugh had Mrs Oldfield, who played Leonora's maid, the knowing and realistic Jacinta, step forward and address the audience in the Epilogue, the import of which is to reopen the entire conclusion of the play:

> What say you, Sirs, do ye think my Lady'll escape,
> 'Tis devilish hard to stand a favourite's rape?
> Should Guzman, like Don John, break in upon her,
> For all her virtue, Heaven have mercy on her.

The most foolish thing a man can do, the actress tells her audience, is to rely on soft words and billet-doux, for:

> In short!
> We can't receive those terms you gently tender,
> But storm, and we can answer our surrender.

The play may then be ended, but we are left to ponder just what will happen in the next, unwritten, act. Amidst the creaking mechanics of the melodramatic plot, it is the more earthy antics of the two servants, Jacinta and Lopez, that strike the contemporary chord, a refreshing counter to all the debris of past conventions inherited by Vanbrugh with the original text.

Curiously, Jacinta and Lopez were to reappear in the last Vanbrugh adaptation of which we possess a text, *The Mistake* of 1705. In the dramatis personae, they are to be found along with Don Felix, Leonora and Isabella, all of whom had figured in the earlier play. *The Mistake* is in no way a sequel to *The False Friend*, however. This last extant play is an adaptation of an early Molière piece, *Le Depit Amoureux* of 1654, and Vanbrugh's version does little to tamper with its basic structure, other than removing the action from France to Spain and completely changing the names of the characters to include five names from his earlier work.

Quite why he should have done this is difficult to say, for *The False Friend* was not a sufficient success to think that he might have been attempting to suggest a sequel. The effect, though, is to stress an interconnection of themes that runs through virtually all his adaptations, and which, in itself, might argue that Vanbrugh's choice of texts to adapt is less casual than has been frequently argued. Although, in particular, the two servants and the father and daughter who share the same names are given slightly different characteristics – Lopez, for instance, becoming a far less assertively rogue character – their roles in the unfolding of the narrative are very similar. Don Felix's daughter, Leonora, is not in this instance to be married against her will, but she is at the centre of a farcical plot in which the supreme importance of a male heir is accepted by all as more important than her own ambitions for love and marriage. Leonora supposedly has a brother, Camillo, whose male existence has allowed the estate to remain in the hands of Don Felix's family. But we learn early, from a conversation with her friend Isabella, that Camillo is in fact a girl, forced to spend all her early life as a boy in order to prevent the estate passing to Don Lorenzo, who has un-successfully courted Leonora:

> CAMILLO: I own you know why both my birth and my sex are thus disguised; you know how I was taken from my cradle to secure the Estate, which had else been lost by young Camillo's death. But which is now safe in my supposed father's hands, by my passing for his son.
>
> (II, i)

She has apparently been content to play the appointed role through childhood, and it is only the realisation of her love for Lorenzo that has brought matters to a head! And so, we also learn that, before the action has started, Camillo has abandoned her disguise under the shades of darkness, to be first seduced by and then married to Lorenzo, who believes he has won Leonora. Lorenzo is, of course, ignorant of the deception, and exults his victory over his rival Don Carlos, with whom Leonora is actually in love; the circumstances of the marriage have, indeed, already been proclaimed to Carlos by Lorenzo's servant, Lopez, in the first act. Learning that Lorenzo has married, Don Carlos asks, 'When, how, to who, where?', and is informed Cluedo-style, 'Yesterday, to Leonora, by the Parson, in the Pantry' (I, i).

The mechanical nature of the response is characteristic of a plot in which the requirements of intrigue take absolute precedence over any expression of human emotion. And thus, when it is finally revealed that Camillo actually is Felix's daughter, unsuccessfully swapped at birth for a boy who had the bad grace to die immediately, Lorenzo takes but a handful of lines to readily accept a different bride from the one he thought he had, and with it the estate that was always legally his, a happy circumstance that leaves Leonora and Carlos free to marry as they wish.

One of the most comic scenes in the play (IV, i) sees Carlos and Leonora quarrelling as a result of their mutual deception over the marriage, first throwing their gifts and love letters back at each other, tearing wig and head-scarf off, and finally melting into each others' arms. It is an action immediately echoed by the two servants, Jacinta and Sancho, who repeat the exercise on a more modest level, before also embracing. As in *The False Friend* and elsewhere, the comic use of the servants is such as to deflate any possibility of an audience taking the melodramatic antics of the plot seriously.

And just as *The False Friend* came complete with an epilogue which suggested the inappropriateness of the narrative resolution in a contemporary world, so this play carries an epilogue supplied by the editor of *The Gentleman's Journal*, the prototype of the modern periodical, Peter Motteux, which brings the audience back from the farcical romances of an imaginary Spain to the more mundane realities of a modern London. Camillo's plot might work in a play, but would most likely misfire in life:

'Tis well the scenes in Spain; thus in the dark,
I should be loath to trust a London spark.
Some accident might, for a private reason,
Silence a female, all this acting season.
Hard fate of Woman! Anyone would vex,
To think what odds, you men have, of our sex.
Restraint and customs share our inclination,
You men can try; and run over half the nation.
We dare not, even to avoid reproach,
When you're at Whites, peep out of Hackney-Coach;
Nor with a friend at night, our fame regarding,
With glass drawn up, drive about Covent-Garden.
If poor Town-Ladies steal in here, you rail,
Though like chaste nuns, their modest looks they veil;
With this decorum, they can hardly gain
To be thought virtuous, even in Drury-Lane.

As so often in his adaptations, Vanbrugh seeks both to make use of the outmoded conventions of the borrowed plots and, at the same time, to point out their absurdities, and indeed, from a female perspective, their cruelties, to his audience. In so doing, the adaptations are less concerned with the dilemma exemplified by Lady Brute in the earlier *Provoked Wife*, of a woman unhappily married to a man who does not deserve her, and more with the particular problems of the daughter as disposable goods at the service of a patriarchal world of contracts and estates. Vanbrugh's particular treatment of plots which apparently validate this use of unmarried daughters is such as to undermine the certainties of such male manipulation. The female servants are always more sensible than their mistresses, the mechanics of the plots stretched to the point of absurdity, and overall there is a sense of a continuing questioning of a society organised along such lines.

Vanbrugh lived into the century in which the issues raised for women would receive far more scrupulous attention in the emerging novel tradition, and certainly there is nothing in his work which remotely hints at the tragic consequences of the attempts at an unwanted arranged marriage as explored in Richardson's *Clarissa*; but his adaptations do represent a stage in that process of a reformulation of the rules of polite society in a way that would increasingly reflect the slowly growing sense of women possessing lives independently of the strictures of their husbands and fathers. In Act III of *The Mistake*, Lopez advises Lorenzo to treat his supposed wife, Leonora, who is rightly denying her marriage to him, as a man is entitled to behave towards his wife: 'You haven't been married eight and forty hours, and you are slap – at your husband's beard already: why, do you consider who he is? – who this gentleman is? – and what he can do – by law? Why, he can lock you up – knock you down – tie you hand and heels'. For his statement of a series of obvious truths, he is rewarded only with a box on the ear by Leonora. It is an action that Vanbrugh was clearly aware would be received with enthusiastic agreement by a substantial section of his audience.

If all the adaptations discussed so far share a tension between the ideological structures of an old world and the changing pressures of a new, it is evident that the overall effect is to weaken them as stage plays. Fortunately, the story does not end here, for, late in his writing career, Vanbrugh took the time to work at much greater length on another adaptation from the French. After *The False Friend* it was to be three years before he offered another piece. In the interim he had been heavily involved in the building of the new theatre in the Haymarket, and had produced only *Squire Trelooby* at Lincoln's Inn Fields in 1704 in collaboration with Congreve and Walsh. This play exists now solely in an exceedingly dubious later version,[9] and it seems anyway to have been something of a gesture towards the new company.

However, by October 1705 the new theatre was deemed ready for use and the company moved back from Lincoln's Inn Fields. The season opened with a major new work from Vanbrugh, who was clearly intent on making an impression on the theatre-going public. *The Confederacy* is the most successful of all of Vanbrugh's reworkings, and it was frequently revived through the entire eighteenth century, with a total of 195 performances. That it has by now become somewhat overlooked as just one of the playwright's adaptations has had the effect of creating an unbalanced view of Vanbrugh's writing career. For *The Confederacy* is more than just an adaptation: it is an undeservedly ignored masterpiece, not just a postscript to his career, but its culmination.

To understand its particular significance, it is necessary to consider both Vanbrugh's choice of base text and his very particular use of it. The model is Dancourt's *Les Bourgeoisies à la Mode*, a play whose very title proclaims an interest in the social aspirations of a new French middle class. It was territory that, in an English context, had been largely ignored by post-Restoration comedy. Vanbrugh's decision to base his play on this text gives evidence of his desire to extend the social range of contemporary comedy; and what is perhaps most remarkable about *The Confederacy* is the way in which it seeks to open up the class parameters of a London world in a way that reflected the changes in the structure of contemporary theatre audiences. With this play, we can no longer talk about Restoration and post-Restoration comedy. It is of its century, and that century is the eighteenth and not the seventeenth; and, predating by one year, as it does, Farquhar's *The Recruiting Officer*, it can be heralded as the first great play of a century admittedly not overburdened with rivals for the claims of excellence.

The novelty of Vanbrugh's intent can be seen from the very opening of the play. Having introduced the piece with a prologue in which the playwright argues his case in the guise of a 'shabby beggar', much as John Gay was later to introduce in his *Beggar's Opera*, Vanbrugh does not take his audience into the world of the beau monde; it is, indeed, the first play of the post-Restoration tradition to be constructed entirely around the lives of characters of the middle station in life.[10] Instead, and ignoring Dancourt's example, the first act opens in Covent Garden with a dialogue between Mrs Amlet, 'a seller of all sorts of private affairs to the ladies', and a character who does not appear in any form in the original play, and her neighbour Mrs Cloggit. It is an opening that places the action of the play solidly in the world of contemporary London, and a London, furthermore, in which the street will assume an equal importance to the drawing room as the meeting place for its characters.

The couple bemoan the hardness of the times, and we are never left in any doubt that the prime criteria on which this agreement is reached are economic. In *The Confederacy*, money does not simply provide a part of the conventional plot material of inherited estates and marriage arrangements, it is central to every aspect of the action, and provides the main motive force for every character, with the sole exception of Corinna, the unmarried daughter of Clarissa, 'an expensive luxurious woman, a great admirer of quality'.

Mrs Amlet is presented as the middle-merchant figure between the worlds of polite society, with which Restoration comedy had been almost exclusively concerned, and the new world of City money, on which Vanbrugh will here concentrate his attention. She trades with the quality, and complains that she has worn out four pairs of shoes in pursuit of payment from old Lady Youthful 'for one set of false teeth and but three pots of paint'; but she also trades with the City. She tells her neighbour that there are no problems about agreeing a price with the ladies of quality – 'all they haggle about is the day of payment'.

MRS AMLET: If they would but once let me get enough by 'em, to keep a coach to carry me a-dunning after 'em, there would be some conscience in it.

MRS CLOGGIT: Ay, that were something. But now you talk of conscience, Mrs Amlet, how do you speed amongst your city customers?

MRS AMLET: My city customers! Now by my truth, neighbour, between the city and the court (with reverence be it spoken) there's not a — to choose. My ladies in the city, in

> times past, were as full of gold as they were of religion, and
> as punctual in their payments as they were in their prayers;
> but since they have set their minds upon quality, adieu one,
> adieu t'other, their money and their consciences are gone,
> heaven knows where. There is not a goldsmith's wife to be
> found in town, but's as hard-hearted as an ancient judge,
> and as poor as a towering duchess.
> MRS CLOGGIT: But what the murrain have they to do with quality!
> Why don't their husbands make 'em mind their shops?
> MRS AMLET: Their husbands! their husbands, say'st thou, woman?
> Alack, alack, they mind their husbands, neighbour, no more
> than they do a sermon.

Here, Mrs Amlet asserts a direct connection between the values of
the two supposedly opposed worlds. The puritan righteousness and
the connected insistence on the supremacy of the work ethic in the
new City class has now given way, she claims, to an aping of their
social superiors. This introduces what will be the predominant
theme of the play. The examination of the aspirations of this new
class had been at best peripheral in earlier post-Restoration comedy,
the target for quickly established satirical caricature. In Vanbrugh's
play it will become central and, whilst the predominant tone is still
comic – one of the main differences between Dancourt's original
and Vanbrugh's adaptation being a move away from a somewhat
gloomy account of general human behaviour to a more specifically
located analysis – the satire is more profoundly developed.

In this connection, the fact that the play is introduced by Mrs
Amlet's words has a further significance. Hers is more than just a
prefatory voice from the street – in the tradition of the orange seller
at the beginning of *The Man of Mode*, for instance. She is involved in
the detailed unrolling of the plot at every stage. This is heralded by
Mrs Cloggit's bringing her news of her son Dick in the same scene.
Dick has not been seen by his mother since she denied him financial
help and he swept out of the house, only to return one hour later
dressed like a gentleman and 'tossing a purse of gold from one hand
to t'other, with no more respect (heaven bless us!) than if it had
been an orange'.

> MRS CLOGGIT: But now we talk of quality, when did you hear of
> your son Richard, Mrs Amlet? My daughter Flipp says she

met him t'other day in a laced coat with three fine ladies, his footman at his heels, and as gay as a bridegroom.

MRS AMLET: Is it possible? Ah the rogue! Well, neighbour, all's well that ends well; but Dick will be hanged.

The distinction between Richard and Dick, and the attendant description, already gives promise that the son is himself intent on aping his social betters in the way earlier ascribed to the City ladies. It is a promise immediately confirmed in the following scene. His entrance is prefaced by the address of Brass, 'his companion [who] passes for his valet de chambre', to the audience:

BRASS (*solus.*): Well, surely through the world's wide extent there never appeared so impudent a fellow as my schoolfellow Dick. Pass himself upon the town for a gentleman, drop into all the best company with an easy air, as if his natural element were in the sphere of quality, when the rogue had a kettle-drum to his father, who was hanged for robbing a church, and has a pedlar to his mother, who carries her shop under her arms! But here he comes.

And then the man enters, much like the valiant Dick Whittington in the later pantomime, an updating of the rogue heroes of Ben Jonson's City comedies. Masquerading as Colonel Shapely – all appearance, and no reality – he is a young man on the make, whose triumph in a world in which there is no one to uphold moral values of any kind the audience is, perforce, invited to applaud. Brass tells him that he is in danger of fulfilling his mother's prophecy, and being hanged, for cheating a gentleman at piquet. He has but one way out of his dilemma:

BRASS: Why, if you can get this young wench, reform and live honest.

DICK: That's the way to be starved.

BRASS: No, she has money enough to buy you a good place, and pay me into the bargain for helping her to so good a match. You have but this throw left to save you, for you are not ignorant, youngster, that your morals begin to be pretty well known about town. Have a care your noble birth and your honourable relations are not discovered too.

Dick exits, leaving Brass to arrange matters with Flippanta, the daughter of Mrs Cloggit and maid to Clarissa, the mother of Corinna, the 'wench' on whom all his hopes lie. Flippanta is but one of the strongly developed female characters in the play; and the number of good women's parts in *The Confederacy* not only gives evidence of the way in which actresses were beginning to make a real mark on the London theatre but is, in itself, sufficient reason to justify a much merited revival of the play today. Flippanta is the last in a long line of inventive female servants developed by Vanbrugh and is easily the most interesting, a witty and manipulative schemer who dominates the stage whenever she is present, being more than a match for all who come into contact with her.

Brass asks whether her mistress is yet risen and learns that, since it is only two in the afternoon and she lives the life of a lady, she is not. Unable to deliver a letter from Clarissa's friend, Araminta, Brass turns to the main business in hand, his friend's declaration of love, for, as he puts it quite openly to the worldly Flippanta, 'a woman – and her money together'. Flippanta asks quite dispassionately whether his intentions are honourable or dishonourable, there being money to be made in either case.

> BRASS: Honourably. He has ordered me to demand her of thee in
>   marriage.
> FLIPPANTA: Of me?
> BRASS: Why, when a man of quality has a mind to a city fortune,
>   wouldst have him apply to her father and mother?
> FLIPPANTA: No.
> BRASS: No, so I think; men of our end of the town are better bred
>   than to use ceremony. With a long periwig we strike the
>   lady, with a you-know-what we soften the maid, and when
>   the parson has done his job, we open the affair to the
>   family.

Again, the joke depends on the fact that what will make such a marriage satisfactory in the eyes of Corinna's parents is that City will have supposedly married quality, a situation that is far from the truth. And so, at last, Vanbrugh is ready for us to meet Corinna's mother, as the action moves indoors for the first time.

Oblivious to the fact that it is actually afternoon, Clarissa addresses the entering Flippanta and Brass in the tones of the society lady she would be: 'No messages this morning from any-body, Flippanta? Lord, how dull that is!' Brass gives her the note from Araminta, and the related plot is set in motion. Clarissa and Araminta, for all their social pretensions, are married to Gripe and Moneytrap, 'two rich money-scriveners', and are thus as securely anchored in the world of the City as Mrs Amlet had declared in the opening scene. This lack of real status, and the desire for 'something *plus elévée*', is the bane of Clarissa's life. Her sense of what is lacking is given comic shape in her complaint to Flippanta:

> FLIPPANTA: Methinks you ought to be in some measure content, since you live like a woman of quality, though you are none.
> CLARISSA: O fey; the very quintessence of it is wanting.
> FLIPPANTA: What's that?
> CLARISSA: Why, I dare abuse nobody. I'm afraid to affront people, though I don't like their faces; or to ruin their reputations, though they pique me to it, by taking ever so much pains to preserve 'em. I dare not raise a lie of a man, though he neglects to make love to me; nor report a woman to be a fool, though she's handsomer than I am. In short, I dare not so much as bid my footman kick the people out of doors, though they come to ask for what I owe 'em.
>
> (I, iii)

It is a theme that Clarissa reiterates to Flippanta in the second act when, having received Mrs Amlet's money, she expresses a desire to 'spend some money'. Upbraided by her maid for being in want of nothing, she carefully explains the point of the exercise: 'Quality always distinguishes itself; and therefore, as the mechanic people buy things, because they have occasion for 'em, you see women of rank always buy things, because they have not occasion for 'em'. She accepts Flippanta's assurance that she has 'wit and beauty, and a fool to your husband', but realises that she will not get all she wants until her husband is dead.

In Act I, Clarissa is about to be visited by Mrs Amlet in pursuit of payment for a debt. What she has she loses at her nightly card schools – for, like Dick, her social pretensions include gambling – and her miserly husband refuses to keep her in the manner to which she would become accustomed. Her immediate salvation will be achieved by Flippanta pawning a diamond necklace, given her by Gripe, with Mrs Amlet. Her longer-term solution will be achieved through the letter earlier delivered by Brass. In it, she has learnt that her husband is in love with Araminta. Subsequently, we will learn that Araminta's husband, Moneytrap, is in love with Clarissa. And, with the able assistance of Flippanta, the two wives are easily able to combine forces and to prevail upon each other's husband for the money they are too niggardly to lavish on their own wives; and all this, of course, with a mutual cooperation that ensures that no sexual favours are ever granted.

Dick's courting of Corinna is made easier by Flippanta's arguing of his case but also, significantly, by her independent position with an inheritance not controlled by her father. She has been educated as befits the lady of quality that her mother wishes her to be, and to marry as; but she has thoughts only on love and marriage to the Colonel who has wooed her in rhyme. 'I'd rebel against my father tomorrow, and throw all my books in the fire. Why he can't touch a groat of my portion; do you know that, Flippanta?' (II, i).

Dick's problems, then, lie elsewhere. First, he has neither the rank nor the money of the Colonel he pretends to be; and second, he is in imminent danger of having his true status betrayed by the ever-present Mrs Amlet, keen to be acknowledged by her son. He urges her not to acknowledge their kinship in public with an argument that is, characteristically, entirely economic: 'I tell you it's a city-fortune I'm about, she cares not a fig for your vartue; she'll hear of nothing but quality' (III, i). Immediately before this, he has gone some way to elevating his economic standing, by stealing the pawned necklace from Mrs Amlet's strongbox before she enters. It is worth considering in more detail the role this necklace will play throughout the action, particularly since Vanbrugh chooses to show the audience Dick's theft, while it is only reported later in Dancourt's original.

It was originally given to Clarissa by Gripe, but that he still regards it as his own property – as indeed he so regards his wife – is stressed by the fact that Clarissa dare not sell it outright because her husband has written to all the City goldsmiths to alert them to the possibility. Technically a token of love, it is used throughout the play as a piece of exchangeable commodity – to be potentially exchanged for promissory money notes at the goldsmiths, as was normal practice before the recent introduction of an emergent banking system. Used by Clarissa to alleviate her immediate lack of funds, it is then appropriated by Dick to bolster his chances of marriage.

The necklace is, then, to become more than simply a stage prop. As a love token it is, by its very nature, a highly ambivalent thing, signifying wealth, status and property rights as an adornment around the married woman's neck. But Clarissa has already subverted this reading of the object, accepting it not as something that binds her to her husband but as offering an exchange value that will loosen her economic dependence. Throughout the play, the necklace will continue to connect the worlds of marriage and economic realities in a way that compromises any attempt at a romantic reading of the events depicted.

Even the rather silly Corinna, too easily seduced by the very idea of seduction, has learned something about the unromantic nature of marriage in such a society:

> DICK: Not marry, my dear! Why, what's our love good for, if we don't marry?
> CORINNA: Ah – I'm afraid 'twill be good for little if we do.
> DICK: Why do you think so?
> CORINNA: Because I hear my father and mother, and my uncle and aunt, and Araminta and her husband, and twenty other married folks, say so from morning to night.
>
> (IV, i)

It is a dialogue that recalls the dilemma of Lady Brute in *The Provoked Wife*, and Dick is forced to call upon the full panoply of romance and melodrama – offering to run himself through with his sword – to persuade the foolish girl that their marriage will not be as others. The passage of the necklace from hand to hand tells a very different story.

By Act III, Scene ii, the necklace has passed to Brass, who needs money to persuade Flippanta to marry him, as part of the price extorted for keeping Dick's secret until after his wedding. And then, at the end of Act IV, Dick tells Brass that his plan of carrying off Corinna to marry in secret is ruined because he has no money to purchase Flippanta's assistance – 'I have no money, you dog; you know you stripped me of every penny'. Brass offers to help his friend one last time: 'I'll raise a hundred pounds for your use upon my wife's jewels here [*pulling out the necklace*]; her necklace shall

pawn for't'. It is a plan he quickly forgets once Dick has left him
alone on stage: 'I'll go to Flippanta, and put a stop to this family
way of matchmaking, then sell our necklace for what ready money
'twill produce; and by this time tomorrow I hope we shall be in
possession of — t'other jewel here'.

In the last act, Gripe is brought the necklace by Clip, one of the
goldsmiths he has alerted, and with whom Brass has been attempting to deal. Brass and Gripe quarrel about the provenance of the
jewellery, Mrs Amlet is brought into the argument to tell how it
came into her possession, and Clarissa is forced to deny that it is
hers, only quietening her husband by revealing that she knows all
about his wooing of Araminta with the money he denies her. The
public display of the necklace to all whose lives have been affected
by its progress effectively brings the play to its conclusion; and it is
left to Mrs Amlet, the wheeler-dealer, to reconcile the families in the
common bond of economic realities:

> MRS AMLET: Cock up thy hat, Dick, and tell 'em, though Mrs
> Amlet is thy mother, she can make amends, with ten
> thousand good pounds to buy thee some lands and build
> thee a house in the midst on't.
> OMNES: How?
> CLARISSA: Ten thousand pounds, Mrs Amlet?
> MRS AMLET: Yes, forsooth; though I should lose the hundred you
> pawned your necklace for. Tell 'em of that, Dick.
> CORINNA: Look you Flippanta, I can hold no longer, and I hate to
> see the young man abused. And so, sir, if you please, I'm
> your friend and servant, and what's mine is yours, and
> when our estates are put together, I don't doubt but we
> shall do as well as the best of 'em.
>
> (V, ii)

Doing 'as well as the best of 'em' is not to be construed as a
romantic affirmation of love. Their joint fortunes will allow them
to live as the quality, and Clarissa readily acknowledges that
there can be no impediment to the marriage; for, as Mrs Amlet
declares, 'if madam does not deign to give her consent, a fig for
her'. In a world in which money is the sole motivating force, the
fact of Dick and Corinna's independent wealth will, alone, ensure
the match.

And then the action is concluded with a short and sad dialogue between Araminta and Clarissa, both realising that their plots against their would-be seducing husbands are at an end, that nothing has really changed for them and that, in Araminta's words, 'we are to go on with our dears as we used to do'. At this point, it matters little that we recognise Dancourt as the prime agent in the plot resolution, rather than Vanbrugh. Irrespective of the particular claims, we are left with a conclusion unmatched in any of Vanbrugh's other plays or adaptations. By the clever transposition of a traditionally resolved plot – the marriage of the two young people – on to a carefully unresolved one – the continuing unhappiness of the already married couples – the play leaves everything in balance. There is, formally, a happy ending, but its happiness is called into question by all that surrounds it. At the end of his career, Vanbrugh was still intent on considering the same problematic issues of human relationships with which he had opened it. That he was no nearer finding a solution to the insoluble makes him a greater and not a lesser playwright.

6
Farquhar's *The Twin Rivals* and Other Plays

Farquhar's career as a dramatist is in stark contrast to that of Vanbrugh. Whilst Vanbrugh aspired to acceptance in a world of aristocratic privilege, seeing the writing of plays as virtually incidental to his other careers, Farquhar's attitude was straightforwardly economic. He wrote to support himself. Indeed, formulaic though it is, it is not difficult to see his very first play, *Love and a Bottle*, which was first produced at Drury Lane Theatre at the end of 1698, as embodying aspects of the dilemma he faced at the time. His arrival in England in 1697, after an unsuccessful period as an actor in Dublin, was prompted by the urgings of his friend Robert Wilks, who supposedly told him 'that he would not meet with encouragement in Ireland, adequate to his merit, and therefore counselled him to go to London'.[1] The draft of the play that Farquhar brought with him contains two characters whose significance can be seen to bear directly on Farquhar's own situation: Roebuck, 'an Irish Gentleman, of a wild roving temper, newly come to London', and a destitute poet, Lyric.

Lyric's role is particularly interesting, in that he exists initially only as a part of the subplot set in Widow Bullfinch's lodgings. As such he appears at first as just another of the parodied figures, along with the would-be beau Muckmode, 'fresh from the University', and his teachers, Rigadoon, a dancing-master, and Nimblewrist, a fencing-master recently released from the army after the Treaty of Ryswick. Lyric makes his first appearance late in the second act, when we learn that he is penniless and, unable to interest the publisher, Pamphlet, in paying him for his work, forced to service his landlady, the charmless Bullfinch, in exchange for his keep. What is most significant about this character is that, unlike the satirised teachers of dancing and fencing, Lyric's treatment is sympathetic, inviting an audience to engage with his struggles to survive in a world quite unconnected to the main business of the plot.

Farquhar even provides a longish dialogue between Lovewell and Lyric in Act IV, Scene ii, where a discussion about tragedy, comedy and the relationship between the author and his audience ensues. Lyric's conclusion, that tragedy and morality finds no welcome in the theatre and that the only arbiter of taste is audience approval, again strikes a harshly realistic note:

> And if you would tell a poet his fortune, you must gather it from the palmistry of the audience; for as nothing's ill said but what's ill taken, so nothing's well said but what's well taken. And between you and I, Mr Lovewell, poetry, without those laughing fools, were a bell without clapper; and empty sounding business, good for nothing; and all we professors might go hang ourselves in the bell-ropes!

From his first entrance Lyric is used, then, as a mouthpiece for the aspirant playwright, sharing with Farquhar an undoubted talent for literary parody. That it should be Lyric who will eventually be responsible for organising the entire resolution of the plot gives him an importance unprepared for by the conventions of the stereo-typed characters who surround him. He tricks Pamphlet into being arrested for debt on his behalf and, having once acted positively, is soon intent on bringing the dramatic action to a close. Which, having done, he confidently demands the money he has tricked; but the poet still has a lesson to learn:

> LYRIC: How d'ye like the plot? would it not do well for a play? My money, sir.
> ROEBUCK: No, sir, it belongs to this gentlewoman. You have divorced her, and must give her separate maintenance.

> There's another turn of plot you were not aware of, Mr Lyric.
>
> (V, iii)

And that is it. It is evident that Farquhar's stress on Lyric's role in the writing of the plot, and his final lack of reward are, at the least, to be seen as sardonic comments on his own situation. Lyric moves from being a part of an entire apparatus of caricature into a different kind of stage reality, his fate remaining of minor significance, but one closer to those of the major figures in the play. Interestingly, Lucinda, believing Lovewell to be false, makes an early resolution to marry the first man to ask her, 'a disbanded soldier, or a poor poet, or a senseless fop' (I, i). The poor poet is never a possible match for her; the senseless fop is Muckmode, sent to town to wed her; and the mention of the disbanded soldier takes us to the very opening of the play, and the second character to bear more than a passing reference to Farquhar's own situation, Roebuck, fresh from Ireland.

It is Roebuck who first greets the audience with an opening quotation from Dryden's *Tyrannic Love* (1670), the heroic sentiments of which immediately give way to a more realistic appraisal of his situation:

> Thus far our arms have with success been crowned – Heroically spoken, faith, of a fellow that has not one farthing in his pocket! If I have one penny to buy a halter withal in my present necessity, may I be hanged! though I'm reduced to a fair way of obtaining one methodically very soon, if robbery or theft will purchase the gallows. But hold – can't I rob honourably, by turning soldier?

The scene that follows is chiefly concerned with the very non-heroic effects of poverty on the newly arrived Roebuck, and he is shortly accosted by an ex-soldier, a cripple who has been 'five years a soldier, and fifteen a beggar'. From him, he learns that charity is to be expected from no quarter and that the army will provide no remedy: 'rather turn bird of prey at home'. And such it was subsequently to prove for Farquhar himself. This scene setting is important. As might be expected from a first play clearly designed to appeal to an established theatrical taste, Farquhar soon takes us into the conventional material of post-Restoration comedy with the arrival of the beautiful Lucinda, in love with the friend Roebuck seeks, Lovewell, and her maid Pindress. But it introduces an atmosphere of a harsher reality at odds with the traditional machinery of deception and disguise with which the plot is chiefly concerned.

In the published Dedication, to the Marquis of Carmathen, an established method of attempting to attract aristocratic patronage, it is the courage of the dedicatee that is chiefly stressed; but heroics have no part to play in the theatre by this date. Unable to survive as a heroic figure, Roebuck resorts to the role of libertine and rogue, contemplating murder and robbery and attempting rape. However, once we realise that he has a male counterpart, Lovewell, whose attributes are those of honesty, decency and loyalty, there can be little doubt that the plot will eventually allow these values to transcend the cynicism and despair of Roebuck. Thus, not only is a great deal of the potential of the situation lost, but Roebuck's character has to be arbitrarily altered in order to effect the moral conclusion.

The contrast between the two characters is made explicit from their very first stage meeting. Lucinda and Pindress arrive at Lincoln's Inn Fields, masked, to spy on Lovewell, whom the mistress suspects of infidelity. Quickly assailed by Roebuck, Lucinda resists his advances, only to be forcibly carried off by him. She is rescued by Lovewell and swords are drawn, before the two men recognise each other. Asked to explain his presence in London, Roebuck says that the explanation lies in 'the universal cause of the continued evils of mankind'. Lovewell's interpretation of this is that of conventional Christian morality, but Roebuck will have none of it:

> LOVEWELL: The universal cause of our continued evil is the devil, sure.
> ROEBUCK: No, 'tis the flesh, Ned – That very woman that drove us all out of Paradise, has sent me a-packing out of Ireland.
> LOVEWELL: How so?
> ROEBUCK: Only tasting the forbidden fruit, that was all.
> LOVEWELL: Is simple fornication become so great a crime there as to be punishable by no less than banishment?
> ROEBUCK: Egad, mine was double fornication, Ned! – The jade was so pregnant to bear twins, the fruit grew in clusters; and my unconscionable father, because I was a rogue in debauching her, would make me a fool by wedding her. But

I would not marry a whore, and he would not own a
disobedient son, and so –
LOVEWELL: But was she a gentlewoman?
ROEBUCK: Psha! no; she had no fortune.

Lovewell's decency will allow of the possibility of sexual activity
outside marriage – he could scarcely be imagined in a Restoration-
type comedy if it did not – and his questioning of Roebuck's refusal
to wed is predicated entirely on class terms: was the woman a lady
or a whore? The answer has a real significance for him. Roebuck's
reference to the Fall and the active role of women in promoting vice
is as convenient to his needs as it is conventional; but the play is
unusually ripe with such references. He later refers to Lucinda as
'the forbidden fruit' (III, i), and it is left to Lucinda, discovered
reading in her bedroom by Roebuck towards the end of the play, to
counter the image:

> Man, made our monarch, is a tyrant grown,
> And womankind must bear a second fall.

(V, i)

In attempting to help his friend, Lovewell becomes unwittingly
caught up in Roebuck's efforts to rid himself of the attentions of a
cast-off mistress, Mrs Trudge, who has followed him from Ireland
with the one surviving twin baby. Roebuck's attitude to her is
callous in a way that can be contained in the play only by
Farquhar's conscious depiction of her as a caricature whore, whose
motherhood, it is suggested, may not necessarily be down to
Roebuck, as Lovewell ruefully admits.

Lovewell's attempts to provide for Mrs Trudge give the rather
shallow impetus for the main plot, affording Lucinda evidence of
apparent infidelity on which her jealousy may feed and making it
necessary for Lovewell to prove his worth. Lucinda's behaviour
towards him pushes Lovewell towards embracing Roebuck's cynical
attitude towards sexual relations; and the main action of the play
consists in his encouragement of Roebuck to test to the limit the
fidelity of Lucinda. That we have learned early on that Lucinda's
page is, in reality, Lovewell's sister, Leanthe, disguised as a young
man to pursue Roebuck, whom she loves, makes the details of the

plot resolution only too apparent; and what interest the play possesses depends on the stage business of disguise and pretence.

Roebuck is eventually persuaded by Lucinda and Leanthe's protestations of sincerity and, somewhat unconvincingly, embraces marriage with Lovewell's sister. This is in keeping with Leanthe's pious hope expressed after her first meeting with him on stage: 'Wild as winds, and unconfined as air! – Yet, I may reclaim him. His follies are weakly founded.... How charming would virtue look in him, whose behaviour can add a grace to the unseemliness of vice!' (III, i).

And so, the play ends with matters arranged to the economic approval of all parties, with Roebuck claiming – in a way that totally distances him from the character who opened the proceedings – that only Leanthe's virtue will allow him to accept the accompanying fortune. His final words take us back to the Garden of Eden once more, but in imagery that reverses the burden of his earlier argument and posits the superior power of virtue over vice:

> I have espoused all goodness with Leanthe,
> And am divorced from all my former follies.
> Woman's our fate. Wild and unlawful flames
> Debauch us first, and softer love reclaims.
> Thus paradise was lost by woman's fall;
> But virtuous woman thus restores it all.

(V, iii)

The tension between the stress on libido, drawn from the earlier comedies, and on virtue, drawn from the newer sensibilities associated with Collier's attack on the immoralities of the stage, is never properly resolved. Nor, perhaps, was it meant to be. In the Prologue the title of the play had been explained as offering love for the ladies and a bottle for the gentlemen. Farquhar was attempting to produce a piece that would placate both sides of the argument. In the event it satisfied neither, enjoying the most modest of successes; but it did at least allow Farquhar to announce his presence.

One year later, Drury Lane saw his second play produced. Its main title, *The Constant Couple*, announced a return to the theme of constancy over sexual adventure; but, now more skilled in catering for the conflicting demands of his audience, Farquhar had been able to make the mechanics of plot resolution more lively. What most

obviously distinguishes this play from his first is the firm establishment of a powerful female figure at the centre of the intrigues.
Lady Lurewell, played by Mrs Verbruggen, controls every aspect of
the plot and has the five chief male characters all pursuing her in
the hope of sexual conquest.

The replacement by the female predator of one or more male
rake figures is not entirely without precedent, but Farquhar's extreme use of Lurewell is indicative of more than simply a growing
confidence in the ability of female actors to move away from essentially supporting roles by this date. It represents a move towards at
least a partial transference from an exclusively masculine perspective; although, as we will discover quite early on in the play, the lady
is not in fact the uncomplicated predator figure she is painted. In
order to allow for the transference of the central focus on to a
female character, Farquhar is careful to provide her with an
appropriately moral *raison d'être* for, and conclusion to, her male
scalp hunt. However, the extent to which she commandeers the
traditional role of male rogue/wit at the centre of the plot
machination is still quite remarkable.

Her pivotal importance as plot mover is evident from the outset.
The play opens in the park, that public space that allows cross-
sexual and cross-class assignations. Vizard enters, followed by his
servant. His letter to Angelica, a 'lady of honour' as she is described
in the cast list, has been returned. The servant tells him that she
'believes your letter like yourself, fair on the outside, foul within; so
sent it back unopened'. In reprisal, Vizard plans to visit Lady
Lurewell that evening: 'her beauty is sufficient cure for Angelica's
scorn'.

A recent critic has described Vizard as 'a parody of Restoration
wits of earlier vintage', and it is in keeping that he should thus be
discovered by the next entrant, his uncle, Alderman Smuggler,
reading Hobbes under the guise of meditating on 'some book of
pious ejaculations'. From his very name, it is evident that Smuggler,
whom we will shortly learn is the second of Lurewell's would-be
lovers, will also fail in his quest. They are joined by Colonel
Standard, newly released from the army and bemoaning the hardship caused to the brave men who, once the defenders of their
country, are now unwanted and unpaid.

Standard scarcely has time to tell Vizard and Smuggler that he
rejoices in the possession of a rich and beautiful mistress before the

three of them witness Sir Harry Wildair crossing the stage singing. He has 'newly come from Paris', and is 'the joy of the playhouse, and life of the Park', according to Vizard. Already favoured by Standard, who knows of him as having campaigned bravely in Flanders, he is lauded by Vizard in terms which leave the audience in little doubt as to the traditional role he will play in proceedings:

> Dost think bravery and gaiety are inconsistent? He's a gentleman of most happy circumstances, born to a plentiful estate; has had a genteel and easy education, free from the rigidness of teachers and pedantry of schools. His florid constitution being never ruffled by misfortune, nor stinted in its pleasures, has rendered him entertaining to others, and easy to himself; – turning all passion into gaiety of humour, by which he chooses rather to rejoice his friends than be hated by any; as you shall see.
>
> (II, ii)

Sir Harry joins them and, having entertained them with an account of his martial and libidinous adventures abroad, declares that it is his love of a woman that has caused him to return. Forced to declare her name, Lurewell, Smuggler and Vizard lay distressed claim to her in asides and Colonel Standard leaves immediately in a manner that leaves the audience in little doubt of the identity of his proclaimed mistress.

At this point Vizard realises that the odds are against him – 'he's a Baronet, and I a plain Vizard; he has a coach-and-six, and I walk a-foot' – and plots to involve Angelica in his scheming. He responds to Sir Harry's request to be guided to a 'pretty mistress' with a recommendation of the 16-year-old girl who has spurned him, saying that 20 or 30 guineas to the mother will win her as a whore, and offering a letter of introduction.

Sir Harry having gratefully accepted the offer, the first scene ends with his brief meeting with Clincher Senior, former apprentice to the merchant Smuggler and now anxious to ape the behaviour of his social superiors, having inherited an estate on the death of his father. It is his ambition to attend the papal jubilee that gives the play its subtitle (*A Trip to the Jubilee*); and Sir Harry's conclusion that no amount of money will enable the smooth transition 'from behind the counter into the side-box', for he will always 'smell of hops and tobacco', is crucial to the terms in which the two strands of the plot will be developed.

Vizard, Smuggler and Clincher Senior are doomed to failure in a world of amatory intrigue still governed firmly by the ruling class; and much of the comedy of the play comes from the contemporary audiences' understanding of the ultimate impossibility of them bridging the social divide. What is new is that Farquhar should allow so much stage space to demonstrate this impossibility, for they are the kind of characters who would have been entirely absent from or peripheral to the earlier comedy of manners model. Indeed, their antics are responsible for most of the comic business of the play; but it is comic business that is directed against them, unlike that superior wit principally associated with Wildair in this play.

A second prologue, added several years after the play's first production, talks with the advantage of hindsight of the audiences' delight in this comic business – 'Our plays are farce, because our house is crammed'. And certainly Farquhar works hard to provide such fare. The crowded plot is full of farcical activity, with hidden suitors popping out of every door in Lady Lurewell's house. There are frequent enforced changes of costume, including on the part of Smuggler, compelled to come wooing dressed as a woman.

Apart from carrying a lot of the comic burden of the play, the chief function of these antics is to disqualify these 'lower' characters from possession of the ultimate prize, Lady Lurewell, either as mistress (libido) or as wife (property and wealth). And it is the world of money that chiefly preoccupies all of them, and thus further separates them from the more 'honourable' concerns of their social betters.

Although the characters are all interwoven in the play's action, the subtitle of the play refers to an effective subplot in which the envious younger brother of Clincher Senior, Clincher Junior, attempts to appropriate his inherited estate, and make the jubilee trip himself.

Vizard does not only affect morality in order to succeed in his sexual conquests, as he boasts; he also does so to convince his uncle, the merchant Smuggler, that he should inherit his estate. When he is revealed as a dissembling hypocrite, his uncle disinherits him; only for Smuggler then to be tricked into releasing money of Lady Lurewell's that he has dishonestly held, under threat of having his smuggling of illegal French wines revealed to the authorities. Having provided much farcical entertainment, these characters are all, like Shakespeare's 'rude mechanicals', put firmly back in their place in the social order.

In the struggle for possession of Lady Lurewell, the only real contenders are evident from the outset – Colonel Standard and Sir Harry Wildair, both of whom are clearly perceived as suitable in terms of their rank. That Standard is temporarily without funds – unlike Smuggler, for instance – is less important than his social position. The way in which they are set up as rivals is therefore crucial in ways which relate to the play's main title, *The Constant Couple*.

We have already been given a clear sense of Wildair as a feckless philanderer – and will have this sense reinforced in the second act, when Lady Darling, acting on Vizard's written communication to her that the man intends offering her daughter marriage, allows him access to Angelica. Wildair's attempts to buy Angelica as a whore, even as she has immediately determined to accept him as a spouse, seem less comic now than they would undoubtedly have done then, at least to most of the male audience; but not only does the plot thus demand that the 'honourable' Angelica will eventually obtain Wildair as her husband, it debars him from the position of constancy referred to in the title. The point is made comically clear in Act IV, Scene iii, when Wildair finally succeeds in gaining admittance to Lurewell's house, a trifle inconveniently for the lady, who awaits Smuggler disguised as a woman as a part of the humiliation she plans for him.

Lurewell and Wildair promise to be 'free' with each other, by which they mean honest, and the way in which they immediately interpret that programme of freedom leaves little doubt of Wildair's chances of conquest in a play entitled *The Constant Couple*:

> LUREWELL: Then, plainly, sir, I shall beg the favour to see you some other time, for at this very minute I have two other lovers in the house.
>
> WILDAIR: Then, to be as plain, I must be gone this minute, for I must see another mistress [Angelica] within these two hours.
>
> LUREWELL: Frank and free.
>
> (IV, iii)

In contrast, we infer from the outset that the Colonel, the man of standards, will eventually succeed in winning Lurewell over. He will be the man of virtue in this play, in contrast to the libidinous rake figure of Wildair. And so he will be the first of the male rivals to address Lady Lurewell in the play. For it is to the lady's house that the good Colonel speeds in the second scene, jolted by Wildair's claim to the woman who had declared herself his.

But before he is allowed in, Farquhar shows us Lurewell in conversation with her maid, Parly. She is gloating about the four men she has dangling, not yet knowing whether Wildair, whom she left in Paris fighting a duel over her, is dead or alive. Her announced strategy is far stronger than that of a mere flirt. She wishes to captivate men only to disappoint them: 'I hate all that love me, and slight all that do'. In this she is driven by a desire for revenge, having been herself seduced and abandoned as a young girl: 'My virgin and unwary innocence was wronged by faithless man, but now glance eyes, plot brain, dissemble face, lie tongue, and be a second Eve to tempt, seduce, and damn the treacherous kind'. Her assumption of the role of a 'second Eve' is ironic in this instance. By the third act Lurewell has confided to Parly the actual circumstances of her seduction at the age of 15, by one of three Oxford students who had accepted two night's accommodation at her father's house. She had succumbed only after being promised marriage, and the young man had then disappeared. Her appropriation of the role of seductress generalises her particular betrayal into a grand stratagem to offer, but never deliver, herself to all men. It will be necessary, therefore, for Standard to demonstrate, at the end in a piece of unlikely storytelling, not only that he is inevitably that student, who was forced by circumstances to part from her without further communication, but also that he is not like all other men.

That his task in the latter case will not be that difficult is revealed in that very first stage meeting with Lurewell. Being an honourable man, he has come to confess his sudden change in fortune before confronting Lurewell with Wildair's claim to her. Having no income he renounces all claim to her. The role of economic realism appropriated by all servants in post-Restoration drama requires that Parly respond, 'Faugh, the nauseous fellow! he stinks of poverty already'. But her lady gainsays her, ostensibly so that she can continue to play with him, a claim that is called into question by her aside:

LUREWELL: I'm sorry, sir, you have so mean an opinion of my affection, as to imagine it founded upon your fortune. And to convince you of your mistake, here I vow by all that's sacred, I own the same affection as before. Let it suffice, my fortune is considerable.

STANDARD: No, madam, no; I'll never be a charge to her I love. The man that sells himself for gold is the worst of prostitutes.

LUREWELL (*aside*): Now were he any other creature but a man, I could love him.

(I, ii)

Before he can leave she recalls him, cursing him 'for being so honourable'; but it is his honourable qualities that have already preselected him for her ultimate husband. And, of course, at the end of the play all is discovered and Standard's fears of becoming a kept man melt miraculously away:

STANDARD: You may remember, madam, that talking once of marriage, I told you I was engaged; to your dear self I meant.

LUREWELL: Then men are still most generous and brave – and to reward your truth, an estate of three thousand pounds a year waits your acceptance; and if I can satisfy you in my past conduct, and the reasons that engaged me to deceive all men, I shall expect the honourable performance of your promise, and that you would stay with me in England.

STANDARD: Stay! – not fame nor glory e'er shall part us more. My honour can be nowhere more concerned than here.

(V, iii)

Standard's claim that 'honour' is something more than a recognition of class status is not the only thing that takes the conclusion of the play into the realms of romance. Wildair, having been converted by Angelica's love, has undergone something of a sea change. Before Lurewell and Standard are at last reconciled, he has arrived to tell his friend that he has found a woman whose virtues have convinced him that it is 'unpardonable to charge the failings of a single woman upon the whole sex'; it is the very premise in respect of men that has motivated Lurewell to this point. Wildair will conclude the play with a series of limp and unconvincing couplets that argue for the superiority of women as moral exemplars:

> But woman, –
> Charming woman, can true coverts make;
> We love the precepts for the teacher's sake.
> Virtue in them appears so bright, so gay,
> We hear with transport, and with pride obey.
>
>   (V, iii)

In his Preface to the Reader Farquhar had written of the play: 'I have not displeased the ladies, nor offended the clergy; both of which are now pleased to say, that a comedy may be diverting without smut and profaneness'. This indirect reference to Collier is significant, and surely accounts for the way in which the play's ending is wrenched to produce an appropriately moral conclusion, a conclusion in which the conversion to marital fidelity of the philandering Wildair offends as much against the earlier 'realism' of plays like *The Man of Mode* as does the willingness of a Lady Lurewell to offer a penniless soldier an income of £3000 a year.

There is a clear sense, then, that Farquhar has produced a piece that attempts to walk the fine line between the demands of what is already beginning to seem like an earlier post-Restoration audience and the new demands of a theatrical sensibility associated publicly with the reformers. That the play succeeded, and indeed really established Farquhar as a coming writer, carries with it a certain irony. For, all his final contrivance of the plot notwithstanding, all the evidence suggests that what contemporary audiences most relished about the play was the character of the unreformed wit and debaucher Wildair, played with great acclaim in the original production by Farquhar's friend Robert Wilks – the playwright talking of him as 'so far above competition' in the Preface. Farquhar was certainly astute enough to realise this, for he followed this second play with a sequel, the very title of which, *Sir Harry Wildair*, promised a continuation of his philandering path through London.

Sir Harry Wildair was first performed at Drury Lane in 1701, and it offered its audiences little in the way of surprises. Captain Standard has discovered that marriage to Lady Lurewell is not the bed of roses that he had hoped. His wife seems intent on continuing her campaign of conquests and he soon learns from Parly – after money has changed hands – that he is near to being cuckolded. The good Colonel has now acquired a brother, Fireball, a non-domesticated, hell-raising naval Captain fresh from the Baltic campaign against the Russians, but is himself the same jealous model of honour that he had been in the original play.

Standard greets the newly disembarked Fireball and learns from him that his wife's antics are the talk of the town, something that comes as no surprise to the Captain, who has a firm line on the shortcomings of society ladies:

> A fine lady can laugh at the death of her husband, and cry for the loss of a lapdog: a fine lady is angry without a cause, and pleased without a reason: a fine lady has the vapours all the morning and the colic all the afternoon: the pride of a fine lady is above the merit of an understanding head; yet her vanity will stoop to the adoration of a peruke; and, in fine, a fine lady goes to church for fashion's sake, and to the basset-table with devotion; and her passion for gaming exceeds her vanity of being thought virtuous, or the desire of acting the contrary. – We seamen speak plain, brother.
>
> (I, i)

Lurewell is, thus, set up straightaway as a perpetuation of the model of married women as adulterers borrowed from the earlier comedies. When Standard learns from Parly that his friend Sir Harry Wildair is back in town, his wife Angelica having died a year earlier, it scarcely needs the servant's description of his appearance to alert the audience to the way in which things are likely to proceed. 'He appeared in the Ring last night with such splendour and equipage, that he eclipsed the beaux, dazzled the ladies, and made your wife dream all night of six Flanders mares, seven French liveries, a wig like a cloak, and a hat like a shuttle-cock' (I, i).

A card game has been arranged at which Lurewell and Monsieur le Marquis – a parodied French refugee played by Cibber, as one of his long sequence of character parts – plan to cheat Wildair of his money. Farquhar carefully delays Sir Harry's first entrance until halfway through the second act. He has already come to monopolise the conversation on stage, and when he does finally appear it is in triumph from the card game. The others, including Lady

Lurewell, have lost heavily; Wildair tips all the servants generously and looks forward to spending his money in ways which clearly place him once again a long way from the Colonel's world of honourable behaviour: 'Here's fine coaches, splendid equipage, lovely women, and victorious burgundy for me'.

He is the figure of unbridled licence that he had been for most of *The Constant Couple*, and he ends the second act presenting the disconsolate Lurewell – who is reduced to thinking of mortgaging the estate she had given Standard in order to pay her debts – with a 'French pocket-book, with some remarks of my own upon the new way of making love'. Left alone on stage, the lady opens the book to discover a bank bill for £100, leaving her in no doubt both of his intentions and the value he puts upon her virtue: 'Here's a hundred pound now, and he never names the thing: I love an impudent action with an air of modesty with all my heart'.

The subsequent plot is concerned largely with Standard's attempts to prevent the pair coming together, culminating in Act IV, Scene ii, where a concealed Wildair has to make a sudden appearance to prevent the husband wooing his wife back to faithfulness. Of course, Lurewell never quite cuckolds him and all is eventually resolved. Having first appeared in disguise as Wildair's younger bother, Beau Dapper, and then as a ghost, Angelica finally reveals herself as still very much alive. On learning that she had had it given out that she was dead in despair at his neglect of her, Wildair is immediately converted back into the model of the loving husband, and is able to conclude affairs with a praise of married life.

The conversion is implausible and Farquhar places more stress on the preceding settling of affairs between the two married couples. Angelica counsels that it is 'better to let a woman play the fool, than provoke her to play the devil'. Lurewell proclaims against jealousy, 'for we are more restrained by the scandal of the lewdness, than by the wickedness of the act'. And Standard's bemused enquiry as to how they shall keep their wives 'honest' is otherwise left unanswered. Any real consideration of the theme is submerged in the awkward contrivance of a happy ending. Once again, Farquhar is seen to be conjuring with issues that he is unable to explore fully without, as he feels, trampling on the expectations of his audience. A play that, unlike the earlier comedies, begins to raise real questions about the actualities of married life collapses into the demands of the formulaic and unreal conclusion.

What makes this collapse particularly unsatisfactory is that Farquhar has removed all the 'lower' characters of the prequel, and with them virtually all the farcical business that he had then thought necessary to entertain his audience. Only Clincher Senior remains, having shed his younger brother, and he has been turned into a would-be politician in order to provoke some easy laughter at his expense. By thus concentrating on the world of the wits and their marriages, the sudden contrivance of a romantic ending is even more problematic than in the previous play, where at least there was a proliferation of interconnected plots to divert.

The tension between the worlds of unlicensed libido, represented by Wildair in full flight, and the contractual obligations of married life, as represented by Standard, continued to preoccupy the playwright, however. The next piece he produced, *The Inconstant; Or, The Way to Win Him* (Drury Lane, 1702), stresses the theme once more by the opposing values represented in the two titles. But the play is largely a somewhat messy adaptation of Fletcher's *The Wild Goose Chase*, and the absurdities of the plot are in no way rescued by the play's exotically French location.

What liveliness it possesses comes from the male lead, Young Mirabel, played once again by Wilks; and it is, as always, a liveliness that assumes the absolute right of the single male to philander and the absolute need of the single female to assert herself through fidelity and a steadfast preoccupation with the goal of marriage. He is, as ever, the enthusiastically single male wooed persistently, and naturally eventually with success, by a rich and beautiful heroine, Oleana. The terms of his resistance to marriage are set out well at the beginning of Act III, when he counters his father's bluster in a familiar fashion:

> OLD MIRABEL: How dare you refuse a lady with ten thousand pound, you impudent rascal?
> YOUNG MIRABEL: If you bribe me into bondage with the riches of Croesus, you leave me but a beggar for want of my liberty.

But having run the full gamut of romantic contrivances – including the almost obligatory disguise as a man, and a gallant rescue of her man from a murderous band of bravoes – Oleana finally triumphs. The young hero embraces 'soft, virtuous, amorous bondage' with enthusiasm; and it is left to Nathaniel Rowe's

Epilogue to offer a more honest conclusion to the hero's dilemma:

> Let the good man, for marriage rites designed,
> With studious care, and oblique of mind,
> Turn over every page of womankind;
> Mark every sense, and how the readings vary,
> And, when he knows the worst on't – let him marry.

Farquhar's next play, *The Twin Rivals* (first produced at Drury Lane in December 1702), was his most innovative piece to date; but it was also the least successful play of his entire career. Viewed in the context of the two great last plays, *The Recruiting Officer* and *The Beaux Stratagem*, it is possible to see the play as, in effect, a transition, a bridge from the earlier immediate post-Restoration comedy to the more socially concerned milieu of his final works. The problem for contemporary audiences was that they clearly found the transition difficult to comprehend. What Farquhar sought to do in his new play was to celebrate the continuance of debauchery even as he is apparently offering a critique of it. It is perhaps not too surprising that it left audiences uncertain.

The play's two central male characters, Benjamin Wouldbe and Richmore, are uncompromisingly reprobate figures and Farquhar's intent to bend with what he took to be the new moral tone of the age results in a plot resolution that sees the total failure of their various designs. But the main dynamism of the play centres precisely around these designs in a way that makes the denouement unconvincing and somewhat tacked on.

The Twin Rivals opens in Benjamin Woulbe's lodgings. The morning has passed and he is discovered in the process of dressing for the day. The ensuing dialogue with his servant Roger and the newly arrived Richmore quickly establishes the two gentlemen as pleasure-seeking philanderers, but it also points to a key distinction between them. Wouldbe has exhausted all his funds in his adventures with Richmore and he appeals to his friend for financial assistance. He is immediately set right. Richmore upbraids him: 'Why would you keep company, be at equal expenses with me, that have fifty times your estate? What was gallantry in me, was prodigality in you; mine was my health, because I could pay for't; yours a disease, because you could not'.

The distinction that Richmore makes between the two of them is not that of class or rank – as it would have been in the earlier post-Restoration comedies. Wouldbe's reminder of their friendship has nothing to offer in the face of the blunt rejoinder, 'Friendship! sir, there can be so such thing without an equality'. The new distinction is based quite simply on wealth. Even Balderdash, his vintner (who has taken from him 'the best part of five hundred pounds within these two years'), is drawn to moralise on Wouldbe's extravagance in drinking above his financial station, once he learns that the pockets are empty. In Farquhar's plays economic status is all.

The central plot in *The Twin Rivals* echoes strongly that of *The Constant Couple*. Benjamin Wouldbe is a twin, and his brother is not only a sober and totally worthy character (travelling abroad as the play opens), but is the first-born and the favourite of their rich father. Furthermore, the brother, Hermes Wouldbe, is said to be a handsome young man, in contrast to Benjamin, who carries with him the additional handicap (shades of Shakespeare's *Richard III* in his plotting) of being a hunchback. And, as if all this were not bad enough, the elder twin is also betrothed to the beautiful (and, naturally, rich) Constance, a lady whose very name holds out little hope for the very non-nuptial designs that Benjamin has on her person.

Events begin to hot up when news is brought of Lord Wouldbe's death. Benjamin has a letter delivered announcing that Hermes has been killed in a duel with a German count, and sets about claiming and licentiously squandering his inheritance. The predictable return to London of the wandering Hermes leads to further twists in the plot, as the dead body of the father is made to declare a last will giving the inheritance to Benjamin; and then, when this trick fails, the midwife and procuress, Mrs Mandrake, agrees to bear witness that she delivered Benjamin before Hermes. The machinations of the plot afford Farquhar ample opportunities to satirise the workings and the agents of the legal system, but there is never any doubt that Benjamin's attempts to usurp his brother's place in his estate and in the bed of the constant Constance will be doomed; and all ends as we might expect.

And that it does end with an apparently satisfactory ending from the point of view of the criticisms levelled by Collier and co. at the immoralities of the contemporary stage was obviously one of the major reasons for its lack of success. It is a point that Farquhar makes rather bitterly in his published Preface to the play. The playwright writes, not altogether sincerely, that the 'success and countenance that debauchery has met with in plays was the most severe and reasonable charge against their authors in Mr Collier's *Short View*'. He has taken the attacks seriously in this play he claims, and has 'sought to improve upon his invective, and to make the stage flourish, by virtue of that satire by which he thought to suppress it'. By showing the failure of Benjamin and Richmore's designs, 'I thought indeed to have soothed the splenetic zeal of the city, by making a gentleman a knave, and punishing their great grievance – a whoremaster'.

However, Farquhar observes, this desire for a moral resolution may be what is desired by the reformers, but is patently not what the citizens continued to expect at the playhouse. His attempt to enact the contradictory demands met with a confusion in which neither side was satisfied. The confusion is most obvious in the character of the other reprobate, Richmore. As the play opens we learn that he has seduced and abandoned the pregnant Clelia, and is hot in pursuit of Constance's cousin Aurelia, the intended wife of his financially inferior nephew, Captain Trueman. The subsequent plotting involves persuading the naive Captain that his beloved Aurelia has already agreed to sell her favours to Richmore, and that she will soon be on the open market – 'In a year or two, she dwindles to a perfect basset-bank; everybody may play at it that pleases, and then you may put in for a piece or two'. As a consolation prize Richmore offers Trueman marriage to Clelia, and proceeds on his attempted rape of Aurelia, the frustration of which by the newly enlightened Trueman allows the audience the familiar titillation of the appearance of the dishevelled actress playing the part. Clelia never appears – as Farquhar claims in his Preface, he thought it improper to show 'a lady of figure under a misfortune; for which reason I made her only nominal, and chose to expose the person that injured her' – and in the end Richmore is forced to offer marriage, a conclusion of rather dubious moral probity, given his earlier stated distaste for her.

So if, ultimately, the rogues are seen to be ousted and the morally correct figures successfully settled financially and in potential wedlock, it is actually a somewhat spurious moral resolution. This is something that Farquhar cannot resist commenting on sardonically in his Preface. Having argued, with his tongue firmly in his cheek, that he has done everything possible to appease the reformers, he then offers to take the reader beyond the end of the play. Although Richmore concludes by agreeing to marry Clelia, 'he was no sooner off the stage but he changed his mind, and the poor lady is still in *status quo*'. *The Twin Rivals* is not a play shaped by the demands of the reformers, but rather one that pays an uneasy, and easily decodable, lip service to them. Its real interest, in the overall context of Farquhar's career, lies elsewhere.

Farquhar claimed of his play that 'few of our modern writers have been less beholden to foreign assistance in their plays, than I have been'.[3] Now, whilst it is true that much of the plot lines of the play derive from those of the earlier comedies, it was certainly the most innovatory piece that Farquhar had yet produced. Although the two main plots concerning Richmore and Benjamin keep the action in the familiar territory of the 'beau, cully, cuckold or coquette',[4] the play is also populated by a series of characters from outside the world of wits, gallants and ladies, characters who, whilst theoretically serving merely as plot movers, actually give the play much of its energy. They are rogue characters who look back more to the world of Ben Jonson in, for instance, *The Alchemist* (1610); the sort of characters who had been tentatively present in Etherege's first play, *The Comical Revenge* (1664), but who had been completely weeded out by the time of his final play, *The Man of Mode* (1676), the play which, as Kathleen Lynch has persuasively argued, became the model of what post-Restoration comedy should be.[5]

In Act I, Scene iii, we meet Mr Clearaccount, the steward to Lord Woulbe, in conversation with his wife as to how they should respond to the death of their employer. There is only one topic that concerns them, their economic betterment:

CLEARACCOUNT: But what would you have me do?

MRS CLEARACCOUNT: Do! now's your time; that small morsel of an estate your lord bought lately, a thing not worth mentioning; take it towards your daughter Molly's portion. What's two hundred a year? 'twill never be missed.

CLEARACCOUNT: 'Tis but a small matter, I must confess; and as a reward for my past faithful service, I think it but reasonable I should cheat a little now.

MRS CLEARACCOUNT: Reasonable! all the reason that can be; if the ingrateful world won't reward an honest man, why let an

> honest man reward himself. There's five hundred pounds
> you received but two days ago, lay them aside. You may
> easily sink it in the charge of the funeral. Do my dear now,
> kiss me, and do it.
>
> CLEARACCOUNT: Well, you have such a winning way with you!

The humour of the dialogue derives from the way in which
words like 'reasonable', 'faithful' and 'honest' are counterpointed
by the calm logic of economic rationalism and the occasional
lapse into real honesty, as when Clearaccount talks of cheating.
As the cosy exchange of a married couple whose sole interest is
in financial betterment, it anticipates the world of Mr and Mrs
Peachum in John Gay's *Beggar's Opera*, and it helps to demonstrate the way in which Farquhar was moving comedy away from
the world of the privileged and leisured classes, and somewhat
nearer the day-to-day concerns of the newer, civic members of
the audience.

To the Clearaccounts can be added the rather minor figures of
the goldsmith, Fairbank, and the vintner, Balderdash, for, minor
characters though they be, they bring with them the world of
the streets and of trade. Of greater significance is the attorney,
Subtleman, who arranges for the corpse of the dead father to speak
again; but most magnificently there is the figure of Mrs Mandrake,
the midwife who has not only brought all the young ladies of the
play into the world but cheerfully accepts reward to arrange the
disposal of their maidenheads to the young men who had been her
other clients at birth. In her joint roles as midwife and procuress she
unites the two main concerns of the play, the pursuit of libidinous
sexual gratification and the running of a profitable business, and
takes us as far away from the values of romance as had yet been
done. That Farquhar presents her as not only an utterly corrupt
person, but one who would ape the manners of the social superiors
whose births she had presided over and whose sexual destinies she
seeks to control, makes her a figure who is central to the play.
Confessing to a slight malady on her visit to Benjamin's lodgings (II,
iii), she requests some brandy. Her superficial refinement soon gives
away to a comically open gluttony: 'Here, boy, this glass is too big;
carry it away, I'll take a sup out of the bottle'. And earlier (I, ii) in her
own house, when she is visited by a Richmore intent on enlisting
her help in seducing Aurelia, she readily agrees to cooperate but

shows a commendable, if temporary, sensibility about being paid as a procuress:

> RICHMORE: Here, my dear mother, Aurelia's the word. (*Offers her money.*)
> MRS MANDRAKE: Pardon me, sir! – (*Refusing the money.*) Did you ever know me mercenary? No, no, sir; virtue is its own reward.
> RICHMORE: Nay, but madam, I owe you for the teeth-powder you sent me.
> MRS MANDRAKE: Oh, that's another matter, sir! – (*Takes the money.*) I hope you like it, sir?
> RICHMORE: Extremely, madam. – (*Aside.*) But it was somewhat dear of twenty guineas.

The old wit/seducer figure is here confronted by a new world of trade, their coming together necessitated in a world in which flesh is simply another commodity. Mrs Mandrake – again, interestingly, a female part – is easily the most lively character in the play; and with her placement amongst the other non-aristocratic figures the emphasis of the play is moved down the social ladder in ways that Farquhar was to consider more fully, and more profoundly, in *The Recruiting Officer*. That he was aware of the significance of the move away from the social milieu of the earlier comedies is quite apparent in what he writes in his Preface:

> 'Tis said, I must own, that the business of comedy is chiefly to ridicule folly; and that the punishment of vice falls rather into the province of tragedy; but if there be a middle sort of wickedness, too high for the sock, and too low for the buskin, is there any reason that it should go unpunished? What are more obnoxious to human society, than the villainies exposed in this play, the frauds, plots, and contrivances upon the fortunes of men, and the virtue of women? But the persons are too mean for the heroic; then what must we do with them? Why, they must of necessity drop into comedy.

Conventionally, the (gentle)men are to be concerned with fortune, whilst the (gentle)women have their virtue to uphold, but already Farquhar has begun to be concerned with a far more complicated analysis of his society, one in which the presumption of rank is not all and, indeed, in which the stereotyped distinctions of gender are far more problematic. It was to be in his last two plays that he really took on the implications of these changes.

7
Farquhar's *The Recruiting Officer* and *The Beaux Stratagem*

The Twin Rivals was published by Bernard Lintott in December 1702. Its publication did little financially to rescue Farquhar from the disappointing reception accorded to the play in performance, and it was to be more than three years before he returned to the stage. In 1703 Farquhar married Margaret Penell, a widow with two children. He did so, apparently, expecting that the lady would come with a fortune; but if this was the case then the playwright found himself as sadly disappointed as the protagonist of many a post-Restoration comedy.[1] His remedy for the continuing, and now exacerbated, financial hardship was an equally familiar one. In the spring of 1704 Farquhar enlisted in the army, acquiring a lieutenant's commission. Before embarking with his regiment to Ireland, he was sent as a recruiting officer to Shrewsbury, where, according to the Duke of Orrery, he was extremely successful in 'raising and recruiting the said Regiment'.[2] And it was from this experience that the idea of the first of his two great last plays, *The Recruiting Officer*, evolved. For, if quasi-biographical elements abound in his earlier plays, then here the playwright can be seen to draw directly from his own observations in constructing the overall social milieu of the play. The central male protagonist, Captain Plume, is always a theatrical character, but it is a character that is drawn, perhaps somewhat romantically, from Farquhar's perception of himself in the parallel role. Furthermore, it has been claimed that many of *The Recruiting Officer*'s other characters are based on the 'Friends round the Wrekin', to whom the published edition of the play is dedicated.[3]

There was a long gap between *The Twin Rivals* and *The Recruiting Officer*, with only the brief farcical afterpiece *The Stage Coach* (written with Peter Motteux) to remind the theatre-going public of Farquhar's continuing existence. Unlike *The Stage Coach*, which cost the play-wright a great deal of time and effort, *The Recruiting Officer* appears to have been written in considerable haste – certainly the printed text is riddled with minor, and quite easily correctable, errors.[4] The probable explanation for this haste is that Farquhar had been forced to extricate himself from the army, finding himself drawn into further debt and with a wife short of the expected fortune; and that, as always, he turned to the stage in the hope of some financial relief. Critics have noted a number of small borrowings from earlier comedies,[5] which would anyway be entirely consistent with the essentially genre-driven material produced for the playhouses, but which might also suggest a desire to complete the piece as quickly as possible.

That the play should be set in Shrewsbury at all points to the first important break that Farquhar is making with the earlier post-Restoration comedy tradition. What would have seemed most immediately surprising to contemporary audiences of both *The Recruiting Officer* and *The Beaux Stratagem* was that neither play was set in London, but in the world of the provinces, upon which scorn was so consistently poured by the wits and ladies of the earlier drama. It is the world from which Pinchwife unwittingly releases his new wife in Wycherley's *The Country Wife*, and that is so un-favourably compared with the capital by Harriett, condemned to being carried off into the country, at the end of Etherege's *The Man of Mode*: 'pity me, who am going to that sad place. Methinks I hear the hateful noise of rooks already – Kaw, Kaw, Kaw – There's music in the worst cry in London' (V, ii). Moreover, Farquhar goes to great pains to create a realised locale for his audience, stressing that the action really is set away from the familiar world of the metropolis.

This change of locale is the single most obviously innovatory, and subsequently influential, aspect of the play. Kenny sums up its significance well: 'Critics generally agree that in forsaking the London drawing-room for the country air of Shrewsbury, Farquhar was introducing a new kind of atmosphere into comedy which was to affect not only *The Beaux Stratagem* but other subsequent comedy as well'.[6] It is not just the fact of the shift of location to the provinces that marks out *The Recruiting Officer*, however. It is the treatment afforded the new theatrical territory and its inhabitants that really signifies the final break with the post-Restoration tradition and places the play in an essentially eighteenth-century context that will lead to, amongst other things, the depiction of Tom Jones in Henry Fielding's novel. As Farquhar argues in his Dedication, his intention was 'to write a Comedy, not a Libel', and consequently he writes not from a satirical, London-oriented perspective, but with the sympathy and engagement of the open-minded tourist, the tourist being both Farquhar himself and his theatrical counterpart, Captain Plume.

This stated desire to be writing a comic account of life in a provincial town merits some consideration. Although he is well capable of having a little gentle fun at the expense of both the inhabitants of Shrewsbury and its temporary guests, Farquhar is clearly not writing as a satirist. Superficially, his position would appear to be that of a humanist, offering a generally sympathetic – albeit, warts-and-all – account of the various stratifications of society. And, certainly, many productions of the play have attempted to construct such a model, generally agreeing with Leigh Hunt's 1840 emphasis on its 'gaiety and good humour', and its evocation of 'the clear, fresh, ruddy-making air of a remote country town, neighboured by hospitable elegance'.[7]

Indeed, when the characters are considered in isolation, it is not difficult to see how such a reading of the play can be found. Plume's rival as recruiting officer, Captain Brazen, for instance, has a boastful manner that generates much of the comic action in the play, but he is also presented as a man of genuine, if somewhat foolish, courage, not afraid to defend his point with the sword. Justice Balance, the father of Plume's future wife, Silvia, is again presented sympathetically, and never as the curmudgeonly parent in the manner of, for example, Fielding's later depiction of Squire Weston, father of Tom Jones's Sophia, and a character drawn from the standard post-Restoration stereotype. A similar line of argument could be mounted on behalf of the depiction of all the major characters. Perhaps the nearest that Farquhar gets to depicting a thoroughly unsavoury major character is Plume's Sergeant Kite, but even he is rendered comically sympathetic, in particular by his enactment of the role of fortune-teller in a long and wonderfully farcical scene (IV, iii) when he uses his skills to trick men into enlisting and to resolve the amorous problems of Plume's friend, Worthy.

However, when we turn our attention away from the individuals in isolation, and consider the total social milieu with which the play is concerned, a rather different picture emerges. For all that the various rituals of courtship predictably do much to shape the progress of the plot, *The Recruiting Officer* is, as its very title suggests, as much concerned with the process of recruitment in the town. It is a process that reaches its denouement in Act V, Scene v, which is set in a court of justice, with Balance attended by his fellow justices, Scale and Scruple. They are present to consider the appeals of the various men recruited by Plume and his Sergeant Kite under the terms of the Recruiting Acts of 1703–5. This allowed for the impressment of 'such able-bodied men as have not any lawful calling or employment, or visible means for their maintenance, and livelihood, to serve as soldiers'.[8] Now, given the names of the three presiding justices, we might expect that matters will be decided fairly and with a sense of morality, and, in one sense, this is correct. Jeffares puts the case well:

> The court scene, where dishonesty reigns, offers the audience ... the chance to realise that some of those who are impressed do not deserve its pity. For instance, the man who pretends to support five children is enlisted because he is a poacher. The collier who pretends to be married is accused by Kite of having no visible means of livelihood because he works underground: but his supposed wife clinches this dubious argument in favour of his enlistment by revealing that they had agreed he should call her wife 'to shun going for a soldier'.[9]

The problem with this argument is that it depends on an unchangeable consensus about the constitution of the audience, and does not admit the possibility of the text changing with history. If the scene appeared to offer satisfactory justice to contemporary audiences, it was because ideologically they would have been far more likely to align themselves with the ruling elite of Shrewsbury, represented by Balance, Scruple and Scale, than with the unfortunates at the bottom of the social pile, whom they would be only too happy to have do their fighting for them. Nor, to be fair, does Farquhar very obviously dissent from such a view. However, in displaying the processes by which the actual recruitment of men, and the legal enforcement of this recruitment, occurred, he introduces a political ambiguity into the proceedings. The overall bonhomie of the play clearly suggests support for the status quo, but his detailed examination of the way in which society *actually* operates – a detailed examination which, importantly, was based on the playwright's own experiences – moves the play towards what looks increasingly in our time like a version of realism. Given this, it is not surprising that Brecht should have chosen to adapt the play (as *Trumpets and Drums*), in a version of events that moves the political perspective towards the position of the recruited rather than the recruiters and the legal machinery that reinforces the system. It was also Farquhar's move towards the quasi-realism of the dramatisation that gave rise to the two most successful revivals of the play in the modern period, by Bill Gaskill in 1963 and by Max Stafford-Clark in 1988, two directors whose careers are closely linked and both of whom drew importantly from Brecht in their approach to textual realisation.

The play opens in the market square. Plume's sergeant, Kite, is intent on cajoling or tricking as many of the local population to enlist as he can. The drum beats and Kite delivers his recruiting speech. From the outset, the distinction with the earlier comedies is apparent. This will be no drama of chambers and closets, the provinces of a leisured and pleasure-seeking beau monde; it is set in the public arena and, whilst, as I have argued, the rigidity of the social hierarchy is never seriously questioned, Farquhar does at the very least allow the different social classes to meet and engage with each other. And what follows from that is a sense of exuberance and energy that looks back to the world of Falstaff, Bardolph, Pistol, *et al.*, and their very non-heroic antics in Shakespeare's *Henry IV, Part I* and *II*, rather than to the polished world of wit of *The Way of the World* that Congreve had offered as a final culmination of the comedy of manners tradition at the very end of the seventeenth century.

The plot of Farquhar's new play is much less complicated than that of the earlier comedies of wit and intrigue. We are almost immediately introduced to the play's chief male protagonist,

Captain Plume, Sergeant Kite's superior, a rakish fellow with, as we will discover, a good heart. He can be seen as an amalgam of the paired-opposite male figures of Farquhar's earlier comedies. It will be Plume who firmly controls the initial strands of the plot and his essentially benevolent view of humanity that will prevail as the events unfold. It is a benevolence, however, that does not smack of the new sentimentalism. Releasing the two rustic bumpkins, Thomas Appletree and Costar Pearmain, from their enlistment, into which they have been tricked by Kite (II, iii), he pretends to berate his Sergeant – 'Look'e, you rascal, you villain, if I find that you have imposed upon these two honest fellows, I'll trample you to death' – and then immediately sweet-talks them into re-enlisting. The army must have its recruits, and Plume will ensure that the demand is met.

Plume gets straight to the point on his entrance in the first scene. Asking Kite how the recruiting is going, he learns that he has 'listed the Strong Man of Kent, the King of the Gypsies, a Scotch peddler, a scoundrel Attorney, and a Welsh Parson'. Kite is told to discharge the lawyer – 'I will have nobody in my Company that can write; a fellow that can write, can draw petitions' – and we are left in no doubt as to the likely nature of the recruits. The action may have been moved considerably down the social ladder in this play, but a clear distinction is always to be made between persons of status – by which here is always to be understood property and wealth – and those without. And in many ways this is the key to the entire plot.

In this first scene, having learned that Plume has just become a father as a result of his fling with his 'old friend Molly at the Castle' on his last recruitment drive (a matter that he smoothes over by agreeing to provide for the child and prevailing upon Kite to take Molly as the sixth of his wives dotted around the country), we next meet his friend Worthy. Worthy is in despair. Melinda, who, as Plume reminds him, had been about to agree terms at the time of his previous meeting, has had a change of fortune which means that he is no longer able to court her as a mistress:

> PLUME: Melinda! Why she began to capitulate this time twelve-
> month, and offered to surrender upon honourable terms;
> and I advised you to propose a settlement of five hundred
> pound a year to her, before I went last abroad.

WORTHY: I did, and she hearkened to it, desiring only one week to consider; when, beyond her hopes, the town was relieved, and I forced to turn my siege into a blockade.... My Lady Richly, her aunt in Flintshire, dies, and leaves her at this critical time twenty thousand pound.

PLUME: Oh the Devil, what a delicate woman was there spoiled: but by the rules of war now, Worthy, your blockade was foolish – After such a convoy of provisions was entered the place, you could have no thought of reducing it by famine – You should have redoubled your attacks, taken the town by storm, or have died upon the breach.

WORTHY: I did make one general assault, and pushed it with all my forces; but I was so vigorously repulsed, that despairing of ever gaining her for a mistress, I have altered my conduct, given my addresses the obsequious and distant turn, and court her now for a wife.

PLUME: So, as you grew obsequious, she grew haughty, and because you approached her as a goddess, she used you like a dog.

WORTHY: Exactly.

(I, i)

During the course of the play, Melinda uses Plume's rival recruiting officer, Captain Brazen, as a public rival for her affections. He, happily in pursuit of the £2000 that will come with her, is then the subject of a further plot by Melinda's maid, Lucy, to trick him into marriage with her under the guise of her mistress. But what is most interesting about this opening account of Worthy's dilemma is the language used to describe it. The deployment of the military imagery of battery and siege is conventional enough, occurring frequently in the literature and drama of the period, and, as always, it bears evidence of the essentially aggressively male perspective given to the rituals of mating which are more normally described in terms of conquest rather than courtship. But they have a more particular resonance in a play in which the unmetaphorical activities of warfare form both the backdrop to the action – Justice Balance asks Plume to provide him with a first-hand account of the Battle of Blenheim on their first meeting in the play (II, i), and Farquhar's audience were well aware of the bloody battles engaged on by the British army abroad – and the *raison d'être* for Plume's presence in Shrewsbury. The imagery thus links the two chief areas of activity in the play in a way that is particularly apposite. And furthermore, as if the linking was not anyway sufficiently revealing, it brings with it the third – and ultimately most important – theme of the play, the significance of money in the 'recruitment' of both men and women.

Appletree and Pearmain will shortly be enlisted as a result of an exchange of money or, to put it another way, they will be available to be enlisted because they are at the bottom of the social ladder, without money or property. Molly's services were available to Plume for precisely the same reason, and it is the army's money that will arrange matters after the birth of a son who is rightly referred to by Kite as a new 'recruit'; for, in fathering sons by their social inferiors, the officers will be creating a fresh generation of enlistable men. Plume tells Kite, 'set the mother down in your list, and the boy in mine; enter him a grenadier by the name of Francis Kite, absent upon furlough'.

In Act III we meet for the first time Bullock and his sister Rose. Bullock will inevitably find himself in the army before the play is over, and Farquhar leaves his audience in no doubt about the role that is expected to be played by the sister. She has come to town to sell her 'young and tender chickens':

> PLUME: Let me see – Young and tender, you say? (*Chucks her under the chin.*)
> ROSE: As ever you tasted in your life, Sir. (*Curtsies.*)
> PLUME: Come, I must examine your basket to the bottom, my dear.
> ROSE: Nay, for that matter, put in your hand, feel, Sir: I warrant my ware as good as any in the market.
>
> (II, i)

The somewhat unsubtle bargaining concluded – with a fully developed double entendre that Rose is the only person in the theatre not to comprehend – Plume takes her off to his quarters to arrange payment. Rose re-emerges shortly, laden with trinkets and promises, and it is left to the brother to complain that there should be 'no pressing of women'.

Worthy's dilemma in the opening scene is that the unexpected acquisition of a fortune has taken Melinda away from this marketplace; no longer prepared to accept terms as a mistress, she is now forcing him to consider courtship and marriage. During the course of the play, Plume is to have a rather similar switch deployed on him. For, in addition to Melinda, there is another unmarried lady, Silvia, the daughter of Plume's old friend Justice Balance. The Captain is anxious that she shall not hear of the business with Molly, for he has long-held ambitions for her person:

> PLUME: 'Tis true, Silvia and I had once agreed to go to bed together, could we have adjusted preliminaries; but she would have the wedding before consummation, and I was for consummation before the wedding – We could not agree, she was a pert obstinate fool, and would lose her maidenhead her own way, so she may keep it for Plume.
>
> WORTHY: But do you intend to marry upon no other conditions?
>
> PLUME: Your pardon, Sir, I'll marry upon no conditions at all, if I should, I'm resolved never to bind myself to a woman for my whole life, till I know whether I shall like her company for half an hour – Suppose I married a woman that wanted a leg? Such a thing might be, unless I examined the goods before-hand; if people would but try one another's constitutions before they engaged, it would prevent all those elopements, divorces, and the Devil knows what.
>
> (I, i)

And, indeed, as Farquhar had reason to rue for himself, suppose he married a woman that wanted a fortune! However, Silvia is no easy catch. Already firm in her intent to have Plume, and with a father only concerned that the Captain's intentions are to make an honest woman of her, she sets about testing her prospective husband. Although, as I have argued, parts for female actors were beginning to be less automatically stereotyped, Silvia is still an unusually strong-willed character to be found wearing skirts, a fact that she comments on herself to her friend Melinda. She is frustrated by the limitations placed upon her as a woman, declaring that not only can she 'do everything with my father but drink and shoot flying', but also that the kind of man she finds attractive will not have 'confined thoughts', a quality she has already had cause to observe in Plume, given that she had sent financial assistance to Molly after the birth:

SILVIA: I think a petticoat a mighty simple thing, and I'm heartily tired of my sex.

MELINDA: That is, you are tired of an appendix to our sex, that you can't so handsomely get rid of in petticoats as if you were in breeches – O my conscience, Silvia, hadst thou been a man, thou hadst been the greatest rake in Christendom.

SILVIA: I should endeavour to know the world, which a man can never do thoroughly without half a hundred friendships, and as many amours. But now I think on it, how stands your affair with Mr Worthy?

(I, ii)

Silvia's question leads an audience to make the obvious comparison between both the two men and the two women. All the interest in the resolution of the plot is with Silvia and Plume. In contrast, Worthy is about as dull a character as his name might suggest and Melinda a conventionally flirtatious woman whose despair at the lack of diversion in Shrewsbury would have seemed somewhat provincial to a London audience. And the contrast is quite deliberate. Farquhar is interested in liberating the 'courtship' of Silvia and Plume from the conventional male/female demarcations of the earlier drama. Thus, Silvia's desire to be rid of her petticoats is soon fulfilled, as the playwright has her disguise herself as a would-be recruit to be enlisted by the Captain.

She is then able to take on the role of the predatory lover, a role, as she has ruefully remarked, usually reserved for the male. Furthermore – in the breeches role – she finds herself well on the way to becoming the rake that Melinda had jibed her about; for, to persuade her to enlist with him, Plume assigns Rose to the disguised Silvia as a bed companion, an offer she accepts, having first asked for assurance that Rose is still a virgin.

PLUME: I can't tell you how you can be certified in that point, till you try, but upon my honour she may be a vestal for ought that I know to the contrary....

SILVIA: So you only want an opportunity for accomplishing your designs upon her?

PLUME: Not at all, I have already gained my ends, which were only the drawing in one or two of her followers.... So kiss the prettiest country wenches, and you are sure of listing the lustiest fellows. Some people may call this artifice, but I term it stratagem.

(IV, i)

Plume's is a rather dubious rationalisation. His stratagem is certainly seen to work in the play, but he has already admitted that only the jealous intervention of his landlady had prevented him from coupling with Rose; and he tells the disguised Silvia that the tedium of recruiting must be alleviated with some pleasure. However, the arrangement does ensure that Rose remains unmolested and that Silvia is able to share quarters with the Captain, the better to consider the conduct of her future husband.

The ambiguity is crucial, for it allows Farquhar to present Plume as both the dashing rake and as the faithful lover, if only during the course of this play's narrative in the latter case. Having relinquished all claim to Rose, he assures the disguised Silvia, 'I am not that rake that the world imagines, I have got an air of freedom, which people mistake for lewdness in me, as they mistake formality in others for religion' (IV, i). The significance of this is directly related to the paralleling of Silvia and Melinda's change of fortune. Worthy starts the play aware of the reason for Melinda's refusal to be bought as a mistress. The first meeting between Justice Balance and Captain Plume (II, i) is dominated by the father's attempts to ensure that the recruiting officer's intentions are honourable: 'would you not debauch my daughter if you could?' He stresses his willingness for the pair to be married, telling Plume that she will come with £1500. However, the following scene brings the news that Balance's son and heir has died, and Silvia learns that she will inherit his estate. The father undergoes a rapid change of heart:

I liked him well enough for a bare son-in-law, I don't approve of him for an heir to my estate and family, fifteen hundred pound, indeed, I might trust in his hands, and it might do the young fellow a kindness, but ... twelve hundred pound a year would ruin him, quite turn his brain. A Captain of Foot worth twelve hundred pound a year.

(II, ii)

Silvia is sent to the country and away from temptation. However, the impending change of fortune makes no difference to her. Again, the audience is directed to regard her more sympathetically than Melinda, who is actually quite reasonably intent on making Worthy jealous as a punishment for what she now regards as his previously ungallant behaviour, ungallant behaviour which, in their first meeting in the play (I, ii), Silvia tells Melinda she had, in fact, actively encouraged – unlike her own determination for marriage – and the pair fall out over the accusation. Having accepted her father's declaration that he will not marry her against her will, and having given her promise that she will not marry against his, she then resorts to disguise and returns to the fray as the appropriately named Jack Wilfull.

From this point, the disguised Silvia is firmly in control of the plot. Having agreed to be recruited by Plume, she is single-mindedly determined to 'recruit' her man. There is little doubt about the outcome. Having ensured that Melinda and Worthy will marry, despite the various machinations of Captain Brazen and the lady's servant, Lucy, Farquhar allows Justice Balance to discover that he has forced his own daughter to enlist. However, Silvia is not, of course, without the ability to maintain herself financially and, her discharge having generously been granted by Plume, the pair receive the blessings of the father. It is left to Plume first to take care of Rose, by having her engaged as a servant by Silvia, and then to resign from the service, handing over to Brazen the 20 recruits he has enlisted in place of the £20,000 he had hoped for by marrying Sylvia. The related themes of recruitment, marriage and money are thus brought neatly together at the end.

A theatre audience can easily be brought to accept the brisk way in which Farquhar achieves his resolution; it is, after all, a comedy. However, it is a conclusion that is arrived at by largely glossing over the fates of the play's more minor characters, those unfortunates whose future will not lie in financially comfortable marriages, but in foreign, and bloody, fields of war. The first man to be produced before the court of justice to appeal against his enlistment, for instance, may be thought to have a very different perspective on the outcome. Denied a voice in the scene by Farquhar, his circumstances are presented in as bad a light as possible by Kite and Plume, and vainly protested by his wife. Learning from her that he has five children to support, Justice Scale is for letting the man go, until he is informed that he supports them by the unlawful activity of poaching. Plume reinforces the case against him by arguing that sending the man away will prevent the wife from producing further children to be a burden on the parish; at which point the wife denies the validity of his argument in a way which condemns both of them:

> WIFE: Look'e, Mr Captain, the parish shall get nothing by send-
> ing him away, for I won't lose my teeming-time if there be a
> man left in the parish.
> BALANCE: Send that woman to the House of Correction – and the
> man –
> KITE: I'll take care of him, if you please. (*Takes the man down.*)
>
> (V, v)

This emphasis on the way in which class interests determine the fate of individual characters is to be found in all the events concerning recruitment, although, of course, it was not very likely to have been perceived as a problem by early-eighteenth-century audiences. But it is something quite new and it is something that assumed a larger importance as the play's production history has moved towards the present day. When Bill Gaskill directed the play for the National Theatre (the first London production it had received for 20 years), he did so with an awareness that this tension could have a very contemporary relevance. He originally thought about setting it in the First World War, a thought that was frustrated by Joan Littlewood's *Oh What A Lovely War*. Looking back on the production, he is clear about why he decided to direct the play:

> I wanted to do a Restoration comedy that was *about* something, and certainly in the recruiting episodes themselves the play offers a kind of socially-critical documentation which goes far beyond that of any other Restoration comedy. And, of course, Farquhar does deal with the problems of working-class people in a way that no other Restoration writer attempted. I think this is the core of the play.[10]

That Gaskill can, correctly, find a reading of the play that would have seemed absurd to Farquhar's contemporaries – and, indeed, sadly still does seem to many modern critics – is the real measure of the play's move towards realism. It is not that the playwright wished to present a propagandist piece – far from it – but rather that in depicting the practicalities of recruitment, he introduces the possibility of seeing events from more than one class perspective. The plot resolutions satisfactorily reinforce the status quo, but the differing outcomes given to different individuals, and the way in which they are seen to be achieved, have come to seem increasingly significant.

This sense of a society with opposed class interests received a more formal recognition in what was to be Farquhar's last play, *The Beaux Stratagem*, which opened at the Queen's Theatre in the Haymarket in March 1707. Not only are there two socially distinct groups of characters, but the play moves between two carefully defined locales, each of which is the specific property of one of those groups. The play opens in the courtyard of an inn, and it is not until the second act that the action is transferred to the more traditional arena of the country house. Furthermore, the action alternates between inn and country house in an absolutely regular pattern, until after the first scene of the final act, when the ultimate supremacy of the landed and would-be landed class is confirmed in their capture of the stage space.

The first characters we are confronted with in the play are then, as in *The Recruiting Officer*, not the beaux and ladies of earlier comedy, but figures from the lower orders, in this instance the landlord, Boniface, and his daughter, Cherry. The way in which the inn will operate in the play is immediately apparent, as the pair bustle around to prepare themselves for the coach passengers from whom their income derives. It provides an arena in which the two social groupings can meet. Its importance is confirmed by the immediate arrival of what we soon discover are two down-on-their-luck fortune hunters, Aimwell and Archer. Having spent their small fortunes in London, they arrive in yet another provincial town (in this case, Lichfield), Archer pretending to be the servant to Aimwell, a transfer of roles that they intend to reverse in the next town they visit should they not be successful in hooking a rich wife on this occasion. Archer's appropriation of the role of servant allows him immediately to make sexual advances to the very interested Cherry, but more importantly creates a narrative link in the play between the two social worlds.

The world of the inn has its underside, however. We soon learn that it is the meeting place for a group of highwaymen with whom Boniface is economically linked; his income from the coach passengers thus has a double chance of success. Unable to discover anything about the two newcomers, and having taken custody of a chest containing £200 from Aimwell, given to establish his credibility as a rich young man, the innkeeper immediately believes them to be rival highwaymen, and plans to turn them over to the law for a reward. His daughter is enjoined to ply the servant with drink, and if necessary with her person, to find the truth of it: 'This landlord of mine, for I think I can call him no more, would betray his guest, and debauch his daughter into the bargain – by a footman too!' It is an interesting mistake given their ambitions in the town, for, as their names indicate, they certainly intend to hunt a fortune.

Boniface is easily pumped for information, and we learn that in the nearby house lives Lady Bountiful, a rich widow who spends half her income of £1000 a year on charitable work among the local sick and needy. But, inevitably, there is more:

> AIMWELL: Has the Lady been any other way useful in her generation?
> BONIFACE: Yes, sir. She has a daughter by Sir Charles, the finest woman in all our country, and the greatest fortune. She has a son too by her first husband Squire Sullen, who married a fine lady from London the other day.
>
> (I, i)

It requires little imagination to predict that Aimwell will soon be successfully paying court to the daughter, for, as he says to Archer on his way to make a first acquaintance with her at the church service (II, ii), 'no woman can be a beauty without a fortune'.

No sooner has the first act ended, with Archer propositioning Cherry, than we are transported to the house of Lady Bountiful, where the woman of beauty and fortune, Dorinda, is in conversation with her sister-in-law, the newly married Mrs Sullen. It is a conversation that is opened, innocently enough, by Dorinda's question, 'are you for Church this morning?'; but it is a query that allows Farquhar immediately to establish a number of key distinctions between the two women. Dorinda is of a rural world in which church attendance is a key event in the social calendar. It will, indeed, be where she will meet her future husband, Archer, and its significance in the life of the community is recognised by him in his decision to go looking for a rich wife there. It will also, of course, be the place where the marriage ceremony is performed.

But for Mrs Sullen it has quite different connotations. She associates it with a set of 'Country pleasures! Racks and torments' that she is forced to endure by her husband, and tells Dorinda that had her parents anticipated a married life outside London for her they would have 'early instructed me in the rural accomplishments of drinking fat ale, playing at whist, and smoking tobacco with my husband'. Her views link her very obviously with those of characters who inhabited the earlier comedies. Her distaste for rural life is, however, but a part of her unhappiness. Her husband is the real problem, as she quickly makes clear.

In his depiction of Mrs Sullen, Farquhar picks up where Vanbrugh had left off with the dilemma of Lady Brute in *The Relapse*. Her husband is a drunken sot who cares nothing for her, carefully avoiding her company and the necessity of communicating with her: 'There's some diversion in a talking blockhead; and since a woman must wear chains, I would have the pleasure of hearing them rattle a little', she tells Dorinda, and her comically grotesque description of her husband's belated possession of the marital bed is confirmed by the arrival of the sore-headed man himself:

> He came home this morning at his usual hour of four, wakened me out of a sweet dream of something else, by tumbling over the tea-table, which he broke all to pieces, after his man and he had rowled around the room like sick passengers in a storm, he comes flounce into bed, dead as a salmon into a fishmonger's basket; his feet cold as ice, his breath hot as a furnace, and his hands and his face as greasy as his flannel night-cap – Oh Matrimony – He tosses up the clothes with a barbarous swing over his shoulders, disorders the whole economy of my bed, leaves me half naked, and my whole night's comfort is the tuneable serenade of that wakeful nightingale, his nose.
>
> (II, i)

In Mrs Sullen, Farquhar has created one of his most remarkable roles, and it is her continual cry for help that dominates the action of the play. That the best lines of the play should be given to a female character signifies more than simply a growing awareness of the potential for defining the actress's role as not automatically a passive foil to the male leads – a steady development through the entire period. The particular circumstances of her marriage are used by the playwright to question the more general problematics of marriage as an institution. A comparison with the outcome of the courtship of Aimwell and Dorinda makes the point well. Their eyes will, inevitably, meet at the church service, and it will be a case of love at first glance. Aimwell will court her under the guise of his older brother, the rich inheritor of their father's estate, and Dorinda will be brought to consent to marriage. At which point, the honourable side of her lover will take precedence. His confession is met with a romantic rather than a materialistic response, however:

> AIMWELL: I am no lord, but a poor needy man, come with a mean, a scandalous design to prey upon your fortune:– but the beauties of your mind have so won me from my self that, like a trusty servant, I prefer the interest of my mistress to my own.
>
> DORINDA: ... Pray, Sir, who are you?
>
> AIMWELL: Brother to the man whose title I usurped, but stranger to his honour or his fortune.
>
> DORINDA: Matchless honesty – Once I was proud, Sir, of your wealth and title, but now am prouder that you want it: now I can show my love was justly levelled, and had no aim but love.
>
> (V, iv)

Conveniently, it is soon discovered that Sir Charles Freeman, Mrs Sullen's brother, has arrived with news that the older brother has died, and that Aimwell is actually entitled to the estate to which he had pretended possession; and the happy ending for this couple will, as is customary, combine the demands of the heart with the realities of property and wealth. Aimwell, suddenly enriched, learns that his future wife brings with her £10,000. By no coincidence whatever, this is precisely the same amount that Mrs Sullen tells Dorinda (and the audience) in the second scene of the play that she had brought to Sullen on *their* marriage: 'I brought your brother ten thousand pounds, out of which I might expect some pretty things, called pleasures'. By this deliberate juxtaposition, Farquhar is presenting his audience with two different views of marriage, both of which are firmly located within an economic framework – after all, Aimwell's stated aim was to marry a rich wife, and not to fall in love.

Dorinda and Aimwell can be allowed to slip quietly off into a romantic partnership – unquestioned by Farquhar because the play's narrative ends before the actual marriage – whilst that of the Sullens, a coupling of mutual antipathy, becomes more and more the centre of interest of the entire play. It is not that there were not married couples in the earlier comedies – and certainly there was adultery aplenty – but nowhere previously had the predicament of a Mrs Sullen, trapped by the inflexibilities of contemporary marriage laws, received such a full and, indeed, sympathetic treatment. So intent is Farquhar on pursuing the theme that by the end of the third act he has Mrs Sullen quoting passages from John Milton's *Doctrine and Discipline of Divorce*, a tract written in 1643 which argued the case for divorce in the case of unsatisfactory alliances.[11]

It is a theme that Mrs Sullen enlarges on in the opening scene of the fourth act, a continuation of the action that had concluded the previous act. Musing on the fact that her country has a female ruler (Queen Anne, whose power as a woman is stressed in the play's Prologue), she puts her own situation in the larger context of all women in her society: 'Were I born a humble Turk, where women have no soul or property there I must sit contented – But in England, a country whose women are its glory, must women be abused, where women rule, must women be enslaved? nay, cheated into slavery, mocked by a promise of comfortable society into a wilderness of solitude'. It raises the same questions that Vanbrugh had been unable to provide answers for, as is stressed by Pearson:

> Amanda in *The Relapse* and Lady Brute in *The Provoked Wife* are trapped in oppressive marriages by their very virtues, which forbid them to take the only possible escape-route, an affair with a sympathetic lover. Consequently in these plays Vanbrugh cannot find a satisfactory comic idiom in which to conclude the main plot, and in the final scenes of both plays, he concentrates almost exclusively on the more conventional resolutions of the subplots. Only so can he prevent the comic ending from being completely disrupted by the pathos of his unhappily married women.[12]

Farquhar attempts to resolve the problem in a rather different way. For a start, it is not possible to make a comparable division between main and subplot in *The Beaux Stratagem*. Dorinda and Mrs Sullen are always linked, the more so once the latter has met Archer, and found a mutual attraction that parallels that of Dorinda and Aimwell. The two areas of plot in this play are defined in terms of class in a way which is never the case in Vanbrugh's plays: the action associated with the inn, and that associated with Lady Bountiful's house. As I have argued, they are never really separated, as characters move with ease from one to the other, and by the end of the play Farquhar brings all the characters together in the country house, whose values will eventually predominate. He does so in a series of masterly plot manoeuvres.

Mrs Sullen has been using a French count's advances to her in a misbegotten attempt to stun her husband into paying her some attention. The count arranges to hide in a closet in the lady's bedroom. Money changes hands and Archer learns of the plan, and takes the count's place. Meanwhile, a plot is hatched by the innkeeper for the highwayman, Gibbet, and his two associates, Bagshot and Hounslow, to break into the house and rob the supposedly unprotected ladies. All it needs is for Cherry to reveal the details of the plot to Aimwell, who immediately hotfoots it to the rescue, and the stage is set for one of the great last comic acts.

The fifth act opens in Mrs Sullen's bedchamber, with her and Dorinda, as so often in these comedies, in a titillating state of undress. Mrs Sullen responds to Dorinda's taunts about what might happen if Archer were to be present in reality as he evidently is in her fantasies: 'Here! what, in my bed-chamber, at two a clock of the morning, I undressed, the family asleep, my hated husband abroad, and my lovely fellow at my feet'. Dorinda leaves her, and her luxurious imaginings are suddenly broken into by the abrupt appearance of Archer from her closet. The dialogue that follows is of an unusual degree of eroticism and Farquhar is careful to make it clear that even as the moral wife denies his advances, the would-be lover embraces them: 'leave me this minute,' she declares, adding in an aside that only the entire audience can hear, 'If he denies, I'm lost'.

Then, at the very point at which he picks her up, and events would presumably proceed to their natural conclusion, the lady's cries of 'Thieves, thieves, murder' are ironically echoed by those of

the servant Scrub bursting in to announce the arrival of real
'Thieves, thieves, murder'. Gibbet is disarmed by Archer as he robs
Mrs Sullen. 'Enter Bagshot dragging in Lady Bountiful, and
Hounslow hauling in Dorinda; the rogues with swords drawn.'
Archer and Aimwell display their prowess with the sword, and the
robbery is prevented and the highwaymen taken. Archer, having
failed to overcome Mrs Sullen's honour, has sustained a romantic
wound in defending her person and property, and this allows him
once more to press his case, this time to be frustrated by the news
that Sir Charles Freeman has arrived: 'My old acquaintance. Now,
unless Aimwell has made good use of his time, all our fair machine
goes souse into the sea like the Edistone'.

And, of course, as the scene moves to another part of the house,
Aimwell is, indeed, intent on using the glory of his prowess to press
the very much impressed Dorinda into immediate marriage. But the
example of her goodness causes him to confess all, only for it then
to be revealed that he is in fact the rich man he would aspire to be.
Things between Aimwell and Dorinda having been satisfactorily
resolved, Archer being promised the £10,000 that Aimwell's wife
will bring with him, and Cherry a position as Dorinda's maid once
the marriage has taken place, the stage is thus cleared for Farquhar
to attempt to do what Vanbrugh could not: to provide a happy
ending for his unhappily married woman.

Now, it is important to realise the exact state of the relationship
between Mrs Sullen and Archer at the point immediately before the
final plot resolution, for her position is an extremely ambivalent one
for a married woman to find herself in on the post-Restoration
stage. At her very first appearance in the play (I, ii), she had already
admitted to Dorinda that she was using the French count as a way
of rousing her 'lethargic sottish husband', and bemoaned the lack of
opportunity for taking revenge on him in Lichfield:

> it is a standing maxim in conjugal discipline, that when a
> husband would enslave his wife, he hurries her into the
> country; and when a lady would be arbitrary with her husband,
> she wheedles her booby up to town. – A man dare not play the
> tyrant in London, because there are so many examples to
> encourage the subject to rebel.... A fine woman may do
> anything in London: O my conscience, she may raise an army
> of forty thousand men.

The female appropriation of the conventionally masculine imagery of sexual conquest at the end – where raising an army would have been seen to have rather obviously phallic associations – is countered by the unconsciously ironic way in which Farquhar has her use the word conscience. She is a woman trapped in the moral and legal proprieties of her age, able to dream but unable – or unwilling – to act. Thus, the sequence of events in the final act has to be carefully handled by Farquhar. Dreaming of a sexual liaison with Archer, she is taken from her dream into a reality in which Archer offers to take the decision for her, robbing her of her ability to put her protestations of honour before her libidinous desires. At the very moment at which she declares the theft is about to occur, the rogue thieves put in their appearance and save her from herself. Having distinguished himself as one of the braver examples of that 'army of forty thousand men', Archer again attempts to overcome her expressed desire to protect her honour – 'can honour consist with ingratitude? if you would deal like a woman of honour, do like a man of honour, do you think I would deny you in such a case?' His masculine contractual notion of honour, as honouring an obligation, is here conveniently confused with her female contractual sense of it as the fidelity a wife owes to her husband, but again the decision is taken away from her as a servant enters with the news of Freeman's arrival – an ironically named house guest in the circumstances.

There is no single way of describing Mrs Sullen's position at this point, and that this is so makes the irresolution of the relationship between the two the more dramatically interesting. It could be said that Farquhar is teasing his audience, promising them something that could not possibly occur; it could also be said that Mrs Sullen is more than willing to be pushed over the edge into adultery. The ambiguity is something that can be resolved only in performance, and has certainly been resolved in different ways throughout the play's stage history, and in the context of changing social mores.

At this point, Sir Charles Freeman makes his second mark on the play's denouement. Having already met Sullen and found him a totally unsuitable husband for his sister and having extracted a promise from the drunken man that he would deliver her over to him, Sir Charles initiates the play's final dialogue:

SIR CHARLES: I am Sir Charles Freeman, come to take away your wife.

SULLEN: And you, good Sir?

AIMWELL: Charles Viscount Aimwell, come to take away your sister.

SULLEN: And you pray, Sir?

ARCHER: Francis Archer, Esquire; come –

SULLEN: To take away my mother, I hope – Gentlemen, you're heartily welcome. I never met with three more obliging people since I was born.

(V, v)

Sullen then enters into a dialogue with his wife, in which they agree on the fact that they are both unhappily married and would wish to be parted. However, this mutually agreed separation founders in the face of Sullen's insistence that he keep his wife's jointure (the £10,000 once more raising its head). That Archer is then able to demonstrate the lady's financial freedom by revealing that all the articles of marriage, and the various financial bills belonging to her, have come into his possession by way of the robbery is perhaps no more convincing than the terms of the agreed divorce itself. Neither would carry any weight in a world outside the theatre, but Farquhar quickly ends the play before the audience has much time to ponder on such matters. Music strikes up and the dance begins. It is left to Archer to conclude events with an address to the audience:

> It would be hard to guess which of these parties is the better pleased, the couple joined or the couple parted? the one rejoicing in hopes of an untasted happiness, and the other in their deliverance from an expected misery.
> Both happy in their several states we find.
> Those parted by consent, and those conjoined.
> Consent, if mutual, saves the lawyer's fee.
> Consent is law enough to set you free.

The play's final word, 'free', is, of course, extremely problematic. It is a freedom brought by Sir Charles Freeman in a way that has been the subject of adverse criticism by subsequent generations of critics. Mrs Sullen may end the play separated from her husband, but would not have done in her contemporary society. The so obvious trick of the happy ending serves to reinforce the seriousness of Farquhar's theme: that, for all the Mrs Sullens of his world, there was no way out of the tyranny of an unhappy marriage. It is not the only irresolution in the plot. Archer is now in possession of £10,000, the very amount that Mrs Sullen has been allowed to reclaim. Are we to assume that they will now marry, the dubious legality of the divorce notwithstanding. Again, Farquhar does not, cannot, provide his audience with answers. And, sadly, he was not able to pursue the question further for, even as the play opened, the playwright was dying. By the time that the play which was to guarantee his future fame as a playwright had proved a success with the first of many generations of audiences he was dead. He wrote a final letter to his good friend, Robert Wilks. 'Dear Bob, I have not any thing to leave thee, to perpetuate my memory, but two helpless girls; look upon them sometimes, and think on him that was to the last moment of his life thine.' Actually, Wilks already knew that he had more to leave to 'perpetuate my memory' than that. *The Beaux Stratagem* was to run 632 times in London in the eighteenth century, playing in every theatrical season bar one; and Wilks was playing Archer in the original production.

8
Vanbrugh and Farquhar on the Modern Stage

In 1974, Barry Olshen prefaced a valuable survey of the nineteenth-century stage history of Vanbrugh's work with the following, ominous words: 'Vanbrugh's reputation on the nineteenth-century London stage was largely owing to the efforts of the eighteenth-century adapters of his comedies'.[1] Indeed, to compare *The Relapse* with R. B. Sheridan's reworking of it, *A Trip to Scarborough* of 1777, is to be brought sharply up against the changed theatrical sensibilities of the late post-Restoration period and what was, for too long, to follow. All the problems of Vanbrugh's play are smoothened and, despite Sheridan's public objections to the cult of sentimentality, sentimentalised, as surely as was the unfinished *A Journey to London*, which as early as 1728 had been given a suitably sentimental conclusion by the ever-versatile Colley Cibber and performed as *The Provoked Husband*.

The nineteenth century, generally, judged the post-Restoration comedies and found them not so much wanting as offensive and immoral. There was one significant exception to this rule. Having received more than 600 performances in London during the eighteenth century, Farquhar's *The Beaux Stratagem* continued to attract audiences on a regular basis during the following century. Olshen puts the point succinctly: 'Its popularity may be attributed partly to the compromise Farquhar achieved between the older comedy of the Restoration and the new sentimental genre which *The Beaux Stratagem* helped to promote. The principal characters are often made to talk like Restoration rakes, but rarely allowed to act like them'.[2]

The revival of interest in the post-Restoration comedies in the twentieth century can then be seen as a part of the same change in cultural sensibilities that saw the Jacobean tragedies once more welcomed back to the stage. What both kinds of play shared was an interest in the psychological realities of human behaviour and, in particular, in the tangled relationships between men and women. The same year, 1919, saw revivals by the Stage Society of both *The Beaux Stratagem* (at the Haymarket) and *The Provoked Wife* (at the King's Hall); and three years earlier the same company had re-introduced the work of Farquhar to English audiences with *The Recruiting Officer*, again at the Haymarket. In the UK, all these plays have been re-revived at regular intervals through this century, in London and in the regions. However, most of the early-twentieth-century revivals of work by various of the post-Restoration playwrights can now be seen as examples of theatrical archaeology, being produced in the main by such specialist companies as the Stage Society and the Phoenix Society. It was only as the sense of what was deemed permissible on the modern stage expanded towards 1968 and the abolition of theatre censorship – in this instance a symbol of the move towards a greater acceptance of a debate about sexual behaviour, rather than a directly causal event – that the comedies began to find a wider audience. And, specifically, it is not until the 1980s that there was a really strong recovery of interest in the genre as a whole, perhaps because the sense of the celebratory dance of death of the old order struck a resonant chord in the years of Margaret Thatcher and John Major. By 1988 it had become a significant feature of the contemporary theatrical production; the Royal Shakespeare's Swan Theatre ran a season of three Restoration plays, and concluded it with Edward Bond's reworking of the territory, *Restoration*. This was by then no longer an isolated phenomenon.

The history of productions since the revivals early in this century has, however, been strewn with a tension that is central to the work of Vanbrugh and, perhaps more particularly, Farquhar. In a 1988 consideration of the 'current vogue for Restoration revivals', Simon

Trussler went so far as to conclude: 'For actors and directors, there are hard and uncomfortable truths to be discovered and told in these plays, no less "real" for the fact that their own authors were revealingly unaware of them'.[3] In the same article Trussler had recalled his attendances at the Royal Academy of Dramatic Arts in the early 1960s, and his 'distaste for revival after Restoration revival which seemed to epitomise ... style without content'.[4] What this means in practice is that there is always the potential in the works of both playwrights to produce a contemporary equivalence of the kind of sentimentalism that they originally struggled to come to terms with. In such productions, the emphasis is on the wit of the expensively dressed courtly characters, and heavy stress is placed on the happy ending as a confirmation of those character's right to continue in place.

In 1967 Donald Sinden was persuaded by the director Trevor Nunn to play Lord Foppington in *The Relapse*, a part he undertook with some trepidation, having never acted in a Restoration comedy before and with memories of Cyril Richard in the role at the Phoenix in 1947. Modelling his appearance on that of the drag artist Danny la Rue, Sinden later reflected on the part: 'If my performance was to be over the top, so were my costumes – all five of them, and each one topped by a series of wigs that grew in outlandishness as the play progressed'.[5] Robert Warden commented on Simon Callow's hijacking of a 1984 production of the play at the Lyric, Hammersmith, where his depiction of Lord Foppington caused other scenes to 'fall by the wayside in a cloud of wig-powder because the performances and attention cannot compete'.[6] Clearly, such an emphasis on the main comic character will make it very hard for an audience to retain any interest in the problems of the marriage that is the ostensible subject of the play. During its 1967 run, Sinden tackled Noel Coward at a party, urging him to see the play:

> 'Nothing, my dear Donald ...' He beamed, as only Noel Coward could beam. Surely, I thought, that beginning must be followed by '... would give me greater pleasure'? Instead he continued '... would persuade me to see *The Relapse*.'
> 'Why ever not?'
> 'I saw Cyril Richard.'
> Not to be outdone, I replied, 'I am very much better than he.'
> 'No doubt. He was abysmal.'[7]

The jocularity of this dialogue, and the way in which Sinden describes himself as having consciously intended to go 'over the top', are symptomatic of the way in which Vanbrugh's comedies have frequently been appropriated in the second half of this century: as a costume drama of excessive gesture in which the achievement of gusts of laughter from the stalls has seemed to be the entire object of many a London production – including the 1980 National Theatre production of *The Provoked Wife*, directed by Peter Wood, although this could be countered by, for instance, the more ascerbic version presented by Joan Littlewood at Stratford in 1967.

Regional and touring productions have also usually gone for the line of male gusto and female display, and BBC Radio has not been alone in turning Vanbrugh's work into a musical form, as it did with *The Provoked Wife* in 1964 and *A Journey to London* in 1972. David Hare's lively production of *The Provoked Wife* at the Watford Palace in 1973 had both music and a scene of near nudity.

If there is tension between the elements of entertainment and of debate in Vanbrugh's plays, it is evident that modern productions have not always been particularly adept at examining it; although, in a review of the 1992 production of *The Provoked Wife* at the New End, London, Karen Lesley found 'two different plays going on which don't sit too comfortably when put together',[8] a state of affairs perhaps not too surprising in view of the above. However, there has been a counter-movement, more associated with Farquhar than Vanbrugh, and, unusually, its starting date can be very precisely located.

In 1956, Bertolt Brecht included in the seminally important first London season of work by the Berliner Ensemble his adaptation of *The Recruiting Officer*, *Trumpets and Drums*. Brecht kept Shrewsbury as the location for the recruiting activities but, after trying to keep the original backdrop of the War of the Spanish Succession, eventually relocated the action to the time of the American War of Independence. This allowed him to introduce characters who opposed the ruling class of Shrewsbury and their attempt to rid the town of all potential troublemakers through the recruitment; echoes of the Declaration of Independence ring out somewhat unconvincingly, and, generally, what was politically ambiguous in Farquhar's original is made explicit and uncomplicated – including the transposition of Worthy into a boot manufacturer who is anxious that an army be raised (which, of course, does not include him) in order that he can sell the boots to equip them with. Kite is made much more explicitly callous, and the whole process of recruitment is demystified as a conspiracy of the ruling class over the proletariat.

Now, the real importance of this production was that it was a part of a season that first allowed London theatre audiences to observe Brecht's methods in practice. However, it did also have more direct consequences. In 1960, Bill Gaskill moved from the Royal Court to join Peter Hall at the Royal Shakespeare Company, seeing the latter's attempt to form a large-scale company as an opportunity 'to bring the Court version of the Epic style into work on Shakespeare'.[9] The immediate result was two Brechtian productions of *Richard III* and *Cymbeline*,[10] and they were immediately followed by one of the most important productions of Brecht in England, *The Caucasian Chalk Circle* of 1962, again for the Royal Shakespeare Company. Gaskill regarded it as the most important work of his career to date.[11]

That same year he directed *The Recruiting Officer* for the National Theatre at the Old Vic. In a programme that was stuffed with historical information about the context of the play, and notes from Brecht on adapting the classics, Gaskill explained why he had chosen to direct the original text rather than Brecht's adaptation: 'Brecht took Farquhar's observation as the basis of his own indignation at the exploitation of the working class.... It would be false to impose on Farquhar Brecht's statement of the social situation but we cannot ignore in Farquhar those elements which excited Brecht to make his version'.[12]

What Gaskill did in his production, via the influence both general and specific of Brecht, was to take on the subtext of the play, a subtext that had been quietly sleeping during previous revivals. One brief example will have to suffice. In Act II, Scene iii, after Plume has chided Sergeant Kite for tricking Pearmain and Appletree into enlisting, and released the two men, he then more cleverly persuades them to reconsider. The scene then ends in Farquhar's text with the three men exiting on a jolly song. However, Gaskill picked up on the far nastier realisation of Kite from *Trumpets and Drums*, and as his scene ended the audience saw slowly appear, first the pike and then the menacing presence of Plume's sergeant, intent forcibly on making sure that this time the enlistment really did stick. The facade of gentility is allowed to slip, and the audience are made to observe the very real class conflict that is, almost unwittingly, at the centre of this play.

Although much sparser in style, Max Stafford-Clark's 1988 Royal Court production of the same play laid similar stress on the other side of the post-Restoration coin, leading one critic to savour 'the freshness of approach, despite the occasional regret that I was not being provoked as irresistibly to laughter as to thought'.[13]

Gaskill went on to direct *The Beaux Stratagem* for the National Theatre at the Old Vic in 1970, 'no less successful in its recognition of the harsh realism behind the social etiquette'.[14] In a programme again full of biographical and historical contextualisation, including material on early-eighteenth-century attitudes to divorce, John Mortimer, writing both as a playwright and as a barrister, opens his article on 'Farquhar and the Divorce Laws' with the claim that with this play, 'the English Theatre looked, for the first time, with a cool and modern eye on the subject of divorce',[15] and again the sense of an audience being forced to look beneath the surface wit of the play is significant. But with Farquhar, and less surely with Vanbrugh, this perspective had always been available, and helps to explain their distancing from the earlier post-Restoration comic writers. They were far more aware of living in a changing world, and this aware-ness has come to seem of far greater interest in terms both of historical hindsight and of the relevance to our own changing times.

There has not, of course, been a unified approach to the work of Vanbrugh or even Farquhar. Even Trussler worries about the possibility of the imposition of a 'false periodisation' with what he describes as a 'Sort of scruffy-wigged realism'.[16] However, it has become harder to ignore the subtext in production, although many productions have quite successfully done so. The tension between latent realism and mannered artifice was present in the original texts, and is there to be dealt with in production, even if the results are not always that happy in practice.

Having complained of the blandness of Nicholas Hytner's 1992 National Theatre production of *The Recruiting Officer* at the Olivier, London, Robert Tanich elaborates on the problem: 'Hytner sets the action in toytown with model cows, sheep and pigs, and then, as if to rectify the image, introduces some incongruous twentieth-century skinheads'.[17] More surprisingly, John Russell Taylor was able to find a reading of the 1988 production of the play by Max Stafford-Clark – a production which, in its insistent and exciting reduction of the play to its skeletal elements, demonstrated the director's allegiance to a Brechtian tradition – that denied it a political context at all; in a review he talked of it as being 'blessedly free of the social awareness with which he has brilliantly marred many an inoffensive text before now'.[18]

What this means is that there is still an essentially political argument being waged over the real import of the plays of Vanbrugh and Farquhar. The plays can be made to succeed in audience terms simply as unquestioning costume dramas of wit and bawdy intrigue – in which the very real dilemmas they raised, and continue to raise, about class and about gender roles, in particular, are played down. Writing about the 1989 touring production of *The Beaux Stratagem* that opened at the Belgrade Theatre, Coventry, and eventually arrived at the Lyttelton at the National Theatre, London, John Peters talked of the dilemma for such a production – clearly predicated on the economic strategy of ensuring an income from several sources for the same product: 'the director's dilemma is whether to portray the post-Restoration world as it really was or to portray the imaginary world which Farquhar wanted his contemporaries to see'.[19] Peters concluded that, in this instance, the director, Peter Wood, had struck 'an exemplary balance', but the critic's terms of reference are somewhat disingenuous. The real conflict is not that put by Peters, but rather which particular perspective of Restoration society might be foregrounded for an audience, and what, if any, contemporary issues it might be thought to touch on.

That the plays of Vanbrugh and Farquhar might be thought of as suitable material for a touring production is, then, a decision that has both economic and directly political consequences. A more recent touring production of the same play, by the English Touring Company in 1994, offers an interesting insight into the practicalities of these decisions. The set consisted of a painted rural backdrop, in detachable sections for touring, forming a rounded arch with a much-used door at either end. There were no formal sets or distinction of locations, so that, for instance, a wardrobe was simply wheeled on by the characters to hide in for the bedroom scene. The whole action took place in an implied courtyard with no sense of an inn at all. Now, this decision – taken largely as a result of the economics of touring – brought with it two problems in what was actually a very lively production. First, the audience is given no sense of the inn as a conscious intrusion of low life, complete with the promise of its location as a rendezvous for a gang of highwaymen – a contrast which deliberately confronts the essentially aristocratic world of just about all earlier Restoration-type comedy (a contrast which it is, anyway, very difficult for a late-twentieth-century audience to comprehend the significance of); and second, and resultantly, no contrast can be experienced between the different social locales of this first scene and the second, equally undifferentiated, scene in Lady Bountiful's house, precisely the kind of location where an eighteenth-century audience would have expected the action to be initiated. So that, even with a production that did not set out to emphasise a celebratory view of proceedings, questions were begged by the mere nature of the touring venture.

For many members of a contemporary audience, the problematics of production may be more centred on gender issues. The 1993 Derby Playhouse production of Aphra Behn's *The Lucky Chance* provoked much discussion in the interval when I attended a performance; but most of that discussion was concerned with wondering why the male director of a play by a female playwright had felt it necessary to garb all the female characters in transparent dresses that allowed an uninhibited view of the actresses' legs. I have argued that both Vanbrugh and Farquhar initiated a move towards a redefinition of the role of the female characters in their plays, and thus, by implication, in the larger society. Such a move is not always very apparent in modern productions.

For the future, it is not unreasonable to expect that Vanbrugh and Farquhar's plays will continue to receive a mixed homage in performance, allowing the wilder excesses of sexual titillation and costumed elegance, as well as a more radical questioning of the attitudes that made, and continue to make, such reactionary spectacle possible. That Farquhar's is ultimately the more questioning voice, that he was in his life and his work inevitably never committed to the perpetuation of the status quo in a way that Vanbrugh effectively made his life's work, should mean that he will eventually be recognised as one of the really great playwrights. But this is the world of theatre, and things rarely work out as simply as they might.

Notes

1   Lives, Times and Theatres

1. The Act of Union between Scotland and England was finally passed in 1707.

2. cf. Eleanore Boswell, *The Restoration Court Stage 1660–1702* (London: Allen and Unwin, 1932), pp. 134–5.

3. Any historical account will be partial and, effectively, an ideological construct, so that, for instance, my use of the term 'Commonwealth period' rather than the 'inter-regnum', as favoured by many historians of the period, is, in itself, suggesting a particular way of looking at events. Readers unfamiliar with the period could do worse than to look at the following works, all of them excellent in their way, and all offering rather different ways of considering historical change in the period: Christopher Hill, *The Century of Revolution* (London: Sphere, 1969); J. H. Plumb, *The Growth of Political Stability in England 1675–1725* (Harmondsworth: Penguin, 1969); J. R. Jones, *Country and Court: England 1658–1714* (London: Arnold, 1978); Geoffrey Holmes, *The Making of a Great Power: Late Stuart and Early Georgian Britain 1660–1722* (London: Longman, 1993).

4. cf. Shirley Strum Kenny (ed.), *The Works of George Farquhar* (Oxford: Clarendon, 1988), vol. I, pp. 5, 18, for sources of contemporary information on his early life.

5. Daniel O'Bryan, *Authentic Memoirs ... Of That Most Celebrated Comedian, Mr Robert Wilks* (London, 1732), pp. 13–14, quoted in Eric Rothstein, *George Farquhar* (New York: Twayne, 1967), p. 17. Biographical information on Farquhar is also to be found in Eugene Nelson James, *The Development of George Farquhar as a Comic Dramatist* (The Hague: Mouton, 1972).

6. cf. Voltaire, *Lettres Philosophiques*, vol. XIX, quoted in Curt Zimansky (ed.), *The Provoked Wife* (London: Arnold, 1970), p. xiv.

7. Judith Milhous, *Thomas Betterton and the Management of Lincoln's Inn Fields, 1695–1708* (Carbondale: Southern Illinois University Press, 1979).

8. *Ibid.*, pp. 51f.

9. Kenny, *George Farquhar*, vol. I, p. 119. The play was Dryden's *The Spanish Fryar*.

10. *Ibid.*, vol. I, p. 123.

11. Thomas Wilkes, 'The Life of George Farquhar', in *The Works of George Farquhar* (Dublin, 1775), vol. I, p. xii.

12. Madelaine Bingham, *Masks and Facades: Sir John Vanbrugh, The Man in his Setting* (London: Allen and Unwin, 1974), p. 113. cf. also Colley Cibber's rude remarks about the new theatre in R. W. Lowe (ed.), *An Apology for the Life of Colley Cibber, Written by Himself* (London, 1889), vol. I, pp. 321–2.

13. Quoted in an excellent account of the Queen's Theatre by Graham Barlow, 'Vanbrugh's Queen's Theatre in the Haymarket 1703–9', *Early Music* (November 1989), pp. 515–21.

14. Information in this paragraph is drawn from Bingham, *Masks and Facades*.

2   At Play

1. On this, see Richard Southern, 'Theatres and Scenery', in *The Revels History of Drama in English: Volume V 1660–1750* (London: Methuen, 1976), pp. 83–118.

2. *Ibid.*, and J. L. Styan, *Restoration Comedy in Performance* (Cambridge: Cambridge University Press, 1986), pp. 19–42.

3. Richard Southern, *Changeable Scenery* (London: Faber and Faber, 1952), p. 24.

4. Styan, *Restoration Comedy*, p. 29.

5. Sir John Vanbrugh, *A Short Vindication of* The Relapse *and* The Provoked Wife *from Immorality and Prophaneness. By the Author* (London, 1698).

6. Jonathan Swift, 'The Preface of the Author', from *A Full and True Account of the Battle Fought Last Friday Between the Ancient and the Modern Books in St James's Library*, in Angus Ross and David Woolley (eds), *Jonathan Swift* (Oxford: Oxford University Press, 1984), p. 1.

7. Montague Summers, *The Restoration Theatre* (London: Kegan Paul, 1934), p. 60.

8. cf. Bingham, *Masks and Facades*, p. 86.

9. George Farquhar, *A Discource Upon Comedy, In Reference to the English Stage. In a Letter to a Friend* (London, 1702), p. 8.

10. Simon Callow, *Acting in Restoration Comedy* (New York: Applause, 1991), p. 84.

11. Milhous, *Thomas Betterton*, p. 93.

12. Callow, *Acting in Restoration Comedy*, pp. 80–1.

13. Benjamin Hellinger, *A Short View of the Immorality and Prophaneness of the English Stage: A Critical Edition* (London: Garland, 1987), pp. lxviii–lxx.

14. Cibber, *Apology*, vol. I, pp. 233–4 in Lowe's edition.

15. *The Country Gentleman's Vade Mecum* (London, 1699), p. 39.

16. John Palmer, *The Comedy of Manners* (London: Bell, 1913), p. 241.

3 The Moral Reform Movement, *Love's Last Shift* and Changing Sensibilities

1. Arthur Harbage, *Cavalier Drama: An Historical and Critical Supplement to the Study of the Elizabethan and Restoration Stage* (New York: Modern Language Review, 1936), p. 55.

2. Laura Brown, *English Dramatic Form, 1660–1760: An Essay in Generic History* (New Haven: Yale University Press, 1981), p. 4.

3. cf. Edward Langhans, 'The Theatres', in R. D. Hulmes (ed.), *The London Theatre World, 1660–1800* (Carbondale: Southern Illinois University Press, 1980), p. 62.

4. Jeremy Collier, *A Short View of the Immorality and Prophaneness of the English Stage* (London, 1698), p. 1; and Vanbrugh, *A Short Vindication*, p .4.

5. Kenny, *George Farquhar*, vol. II, p. 269.

6. Hellinger, *A Short View*, p. lxxv.

7. Milhous, *Thomas Betterton*, p. 76.

8. cf. Hellinger, *A Short View*, pp. lxxviif.; and for an earlier consideration of the theme, J. W. Krutch, *Comedy and Conscience after the Restoration* (1924) (New York; Columbia University Press, 1961).

9. Kenny, *George Farquhar*, vol. I, p. 499.

10. Dudley Bahlman, *The Moral Revolution of 1688* (London: Oxford University Press, 1957), p. 14.

11. Quoted in Hellinger, *A Short View*, pp. xciii–xciv.

12. Rae Blanchard (ed.), *Tracts and Pamphlets* (Baltimore: Johns Hopkins University Press, 1944), p. 311.

13. Cibber, *Apology*, p. 33.

14. Cibber, *Apology*, vol. I, p. 275 in Lowe's edition.

15. cf. Jacqueline Pearson, *The Prostituted Muse: Images of Women and Women Dramatists 1642–1737* (New York: St Martin's Press, 1988), pp. 39–40.

4 Vanbrugh's *The Relapse* and *The Provoked Wife*

1. Vanbrugh, *A Short Vindication*, p. 61.

2. *Ibid.*, p. 64.

3. *Ibid.*, p. 65.

4. Callow, *Acting in Restoration Comedy*, pp. 33–48.

5. cf. Frank Patterson, 'Lord Foppington and "Le Bourgeois Gentilhomme"', *Notes and Queries*, New Series, vol. 31 (1984), pp. 337–8.

6. Alexander Pope refers to the periwig of Sir Fopling [Flutter] from Etherege's *The Man of Mode* in *The Dunciad*, vol. I, l.167; but the footnote accompanying the reference – 'This remarkable periwig usually made its entrance upon the stage in a sedan, brought in by two chairmen, with infinite approbation of the audience' – refers to *The Fool in Fashion*, and it is clear that he intends to refer to Cibber's portayal of Sir Novelty Fashion, but has then got it confused with Vanbrugh's Lord Foppington, who is clearly intended by the playwright to outdo his predecessor.

7. Zimansky, *The Provoked Wife*, pp. xv–xvi.

8. Susan Staves, *Player's Scepters: Fictions of Authority in the Restoration* (London: University of Nebraska Press, 1979), p. 111; and see, in general, the whole of this chapter, 'Sovereignty in the Family', pp. 111–89.

9. cf. Michael Cordner (ed.), *Vanbrugh: Four Comedies* (Harmondsworth: Penguin, 1989), p. 398.

10. Zimansky, *The Provoked Wife*, p. xiv.

5 Vanbrugh's *The Confederacy* and Other Adaptations

1. Alwin Thaler, 'Introduction to *The Provoked Wife*', in Charles Gayley and Alwin Thaler (eds), *Representative English Comedies: Volume IV, Dryden and his Contemporaries: Cowley to Farquhar* (New York: Macmillan, 1936), pp. 409–26.

2. Vanbrugh, 'Preface', from *Aesop*, in Bonamy Dobree (ed.), *The Complete Works of Sir John Vanbrugh* (London: Nonesuch Press, 1928), vol. I, p. 10.

3. Vanbrugh, 'Prologue. Spoken by a Shabby Poet', from *The Confederacy*, in Cordner, *Vanbrugh: Four Comedies*, p. 260.

4. Milhous, *Thomas Betterton*, p. 108.

5. Cibber, *Apology*.

6. Charles Gildon quotes Dryden, 'If you'll let my son have the profits of the third night, I'll give you a Secular Masque'; *A Comparison Between the Two Stages* (London, 1702).

7. Dobree, *Complete Works of Sir John Vanbrugh*, vol. II, p. 255.

8. Gerald M. Berkowitz, *Sir John Vanbrugh and the End of Restoration Comedy* (Amsterdam: Rodopi, 1981), p. 141.

9. *The Cornish Squire. A Comedy. As It is Acted at the Theatre Royal in Drury Lane, By His Majesty's Servants. Done from the French by the Late Sir John Vanbrugh* (London: J. Watts, 1734).

10. cf. Berkowitz, *Sir John Vanbrugh*, p. 138.

6 Farquhar's *The Twin Rivals* and Other Plays

1. Rothstein, *George Farquhar*, p. 185.

2. Jackson Cope, *Dramaturgy of the Daemonic: Studies in Antigeneric Theatre from Ruzante to Grimaldi* (Baltimore: Johns Hopkins University Press, 1984), p. 92.

3. Kenny, *George Farquhar*, vol. I, p. 501.

4. *Ibid.*, p. 499.

5. cf. Kathleen Lynch, *The Social Mode of Restoration Comedy* (New York: University of Michigan Press, 1926).

7 Farquhar's *The Recruiting Officer* and *The Beaux Stratagem*

1. Although there is considerable disagreement amongst writers on Farquhar as to whether he thought of himself as unhappily married or not.

2. Quoted in James Sutherland, 'New Light on George Farquhar', *Times Literary Supplement* (6 March 1937), p. 171.

3. Most attempts to make specific identifications between the characters and people in Shrewsbury derive from Thomas Wilkes, 'Life of Farquhar', *The Works of George Farquhar* (Dublin, 1775); and, as Kenny points out in her edition of Farquhar's works (vol. I, p. 5), 'a more convincing if equally unprovable case is made by H. Owen and J. B. Blakeway in *A History of Shrewsbury* published in London in 1825'. The Wrekin is a hill overlooking the town of Shrewsbury.

4. cf. John Ross (ed.), *The Recruiting Officer* (London: Ernest Benn, 1977), pp. xxix–xxx, for a discussion of these inconsistencies.

5. cf. Kenny, *George Farquhar*, vol. II, p. 6, for a summary of these possible borrowings.

6. *Ibid.*, pp. 6–7.

7. Leigh Hunt, *The Dramatic Works of Wycherley, Congreve, Vanbrugh and Farquhar* (London, 1840), p. lxxiv.

8. This act, which became known as the 'Pressing Act', had been preceded by the Mutiny Act of 1702, which allowed for the commuting of criminal sentences in return for an agreement to enlist – a further form of 'pressing'. cf. Peter Dixon (ed.), *The Recruiting Officer* (Manchester: Machester University Press, 1986), pp. 14–19, for details.

9. Norman Jeffares (ed.), 'Critical Introduction', in *The Recruiting Officer* (Edinburgh: Oliver and Boyd, 1973), p. 5.

10 William Gaskill in interview, 'Finding a Style for Farquhar', *Theatre Quarterly*, vol. 1 (i) (1971), p. 15.

11 cf. Martin Larson, 'The Influence of Milton's Divorce Tracts on Farquhar's *Beaux Stratagem*', *Publications of the Modern Language Association*, vol. 39 (1924), pp. 174–8. For an account of Milton's thinking see Christopher Hill, *Milton and the English Revolution* (London: Faber, 1977), pp. 117–36.

12. Jacqueline Pearson, *The Prostituted Muse: Images of Women and Women Dramatists 1642–1737* (New York: St Martin's Press, 1988), p. 79.

8 Vanbrugh and Farquhar on the Modern Stage

1. Barry N. Olshen, 'The Original and "Improved" Comedies of Sir John Vanbrugh: Their Nineteenth-Century London Stage History', *Restoration and Eighteenth Century Theatre Research*, vol. 13 (i) (1974), p. 27. This article includes a very useful listing of nineteenth-century productions of Vanbrugh's plays, complete with many details of cast lists (pp. 42–50). cf. also, Anthony Coleman, 'Sir John Brute on the Eighteenth Century Stage', *Restoration and Eighteenth Century Theatre Research*, vol. 8 (ii) (1969), pp. 41–6; and Peter Dixon and Rodney Hayley, 'The Provoked Husband on the Nineteenth Century Stage', *Nineteenth Century Theatre Research*, vol. 8 (i) (1980).

2. Barry N. Olshen, '*The Beaux Stratagem* on the Nineteenth Century London Stage', *Theatre Notebook*, vol. 28, p. 70. See pp. 78–80 for a list of performances, complete with many details of cast lists.

3. Simon Trussler, 'Filthy and Rich', *Plays and Players* (July 1988), p. 10.

4. *Ibid.*, p. 9.

5. Donald Sinden, *Laughter in the Second Act* (London: Hodder and Stoughton, 1985), p. 168.

6. *Plays and Players* (January 1984), p. 42.

7. Sinden, *Laughter in the Second Act*, p. 171.

8. Karen Lesley, *Plays and Players* (October 1992).

9. William Gaskill, *A Sense of Direction* (London: Faber and Faber, 1988), p. 52.

10. cf. Margaret Eddershaw, *Performing Brecht: Forty Years of British Performances* (London: Routledge, 1996), p. 58.

11. Tom Milne, 'And the Time of the Great Taking Over: An Interview with William Gaskill', *Encore*, vol. 9 (iv) (July/August 1962).

12. Bill Gaskill, 'About This Production', in the programme for the 1962 National Theatre production.

13. Trussler, 'Filthy and Rich', p. 23.

14. *Ibid.*, p. 9.

15. John Mortimer, 'Farquhar and the Divorce Laws', in the programme for the 1970 National Theatre production.

16. Trussler, 'Filthy and Rich'.

17. Robert Tanich, *Plays and Players* (May 1992).

18. John Russell Taylor, 'Theatre', *Drama*, vol. 146 (1982), p. 78.

19. John Peters, *Sunday Times* (10 September 1989).

Select Bibliography

George Farquhar

Editions

Cordner, Michael (ed.), *The Beaux Stratagem* (London: Ernest Benn, 1976).

Dixon, Peter (ed.), *The Recruiting Officer* (Manchester: Manchester University Press, 1986).

Ewald, A. C. (ed.), *The Dramatic Works of George Farquhar* (London: Nimmo, 1892), 2 volumes.

Jeffares, Norman (ed.), *The Recruiting Officer* (Edinburgh: Oliver and Boyd, 1973).

Kenny, Shirley Strum (ed.), *The Works of George Farquhar* (Oxford: Clarendon Press, 1988), 2 volumes.

Ross, John (ed.), *The Recruiting Officer* (London: Ernest Benn, 1977).

Books on Farquhar and his Works

Anselment, R. (ed.), *The Recruiting Officer and The Beaux Stratagem: A Case Book* (London: Macmillan, 1977).

Connelly, Willard, *Young George Farquhar: The Restoration Drama at Twilight* (London: Cassell, 1949).

Farmer, A. J., *George Farquhar* (London: Longman, 1966).

Farquhar, G. T. S., *George Farquhar* (London: Fisher Unwin, 1890).

James, Eugene Nelson, *George Farquhar: A Reference Guide* (Boston: Hall, 1986).

Rothstein, Eric, *George Farquhar* (New York: Twayne, 1967).

Stafford-Clark, Max, *Letters to George: The Account of a Rehearsal* (London: Hern, 1990).

Articles

Cope, Jackson I., '*The Constant Couple*: Farquhar's Four-Plays-In-One', *Journal of English Literary History*, vol. 41 (iv) (1974), pp. 477–93.

Dixon, Peter and Rodney Hayley, '*The Provok'd Husband* on the Nineteenth Century Stage', *Nineteenth Century Theatre Research*, vol. 8 (i) (1980), pp. 1–16.

Gaskill, William, 'Finding a Style for Farquhar', *Theatre Quarterly*, vol. 1 (i) (1971), p. 15.

Gravitt, Garland J., 'A Primer of Pleasure: Neo-Epicurianism in Farquhar's *The Beaux Stratagem*', *Thoth*, vol. 12 (ii) (1972), pp. 38–49.

Jordan, Robert J., 'George Farquhar's Military Career', *Huntington Library Quarterly*, vol. 371 (1974), pp. 251–64.

Kenny, Shirley Strum, 'Farquhar, Wilkes and Wildair: Or the Metamorphosis of the Fine Gentlemen', *Philological Quarterly*, vol. 57, pp. 46–65.

Kimball, Sue, '"Ceres in Her Harvest": The Exploded Myths of Womanhood in George Farquhar's *The Beaux Stratagem*', *Restoration and Eighteenth Century Theatre Research*, vol. 1 (1988), pp. 1–9 .

Larson, M. A., 'The Influence of Milton's Divorce Tracts on Farquhar's *Beaux Stratagem*', *Publications of the Modern Language Association*, vol. 34 (1942), pp. 74–8.

Lustig, Vera, 'Interview with Max Stafford-Clark on his Ten Years at the Royal Court Theatre and a Discussion of *The Recruiting Officer*', *Plays and Players* (August 1989), pp. 13–15.

McVeagh, John, 'George Farquhar and Commercial England', *Studies on Voltaire and the Eighteenth Century*, vol. 217 (1983), pp. 65–81.

Mews, Siegfried, 'An Anti-Imperialist View of the American Revolution: Brecht's Adaptation of Farquhar's *The Recruiting Officer*', *University of Dayton Review*, vol. 14 (ii) (1980), pp. 29–38.

Milhous, Judith and Robert Hume, '*The Beaux Stratagem*: A Production Analysis', *Theatre Journal*, vol. 34 (1982), pp. 77–95.

Olshen, Barry N., '*The Beaux Stratagem* on the Nineteenth Century London Stage', *Theatre Notebook*, vol. 28 (1973), pp. 70–80.

Wertheim, Albert, 'Bertolt Brecht and George Farquhar's *The Recruiting Officer*', *Comparative Drama*, vol. 7 (1973), pp. 179–90.

Sir John Vanbrugh

Editions

Dobree, Bonamy (ed.), *The Complete Works*, 4 volumes (London: Nonesuch, 1927/8) (volume 4, *Letters*, is edited by Geoffrey Webb).

Cordner, Michael (ed.), *Vanbrugh: Four Comedies* (Harmondsworth: Penguin, 1989).

Zimansky, C. A. (ed.), *The Relapse*, Regents Restoration Drama Series (London: Arnold, 1970).

Zimansky, C. A. (ed.), *The Provoked Wife*, Regents Restoration Drama Series (London: Arnold, 1970).

Details of Vanbrugh's Adaptations

Original of *The Confederacy* is Florent Carton Dancourt, *Les Bourgeoises a la Mode*, in Francisque Sarcey (ed.), *Theatre Choisi* (Paris, n. d.).

Original of *The Country House* is Florent Carton Dancourt, *La Maison de Campagne*.

The False Friend is complicatedly derived from Francisco de Rojas Zorilla, *La Traicion Busca el Castigo*, and from Le Sage's adaptation of it, *Le Traitre Puni*, which was versified by Dancourt as *La Trahison Puni*. It is Le Sage's version (published in the Hague in 1700) that Vanbrugh uses.

Original of *The Pilgrim* is Fletcher's *The Pilgrim* (first performed at Court in 1621).

Original of *Aesop* is the play *Aesop a la Ville* (1690), from Boursault, *Les Fables d'Esope*.

Original of *Squire Trelooby* is Molière's *Monsieur de Purceaugnac*.

Original of *The Mistake* is Molière's *Le Depit Amoureux*.

Original of *The Cuckold in Conceit* is Moilère's *Le Colc Imaginaire*.

Books on Vanbrugh and his Works

Berkowitz, Gerald M., *Sir John Vanbrugh and the End of Restoration Comedy* (Amsterdam: Rodopi, 1981).

Bingham, Madelaine, *Masks and Facades: Sir John Vanbrugh, the Man in his Setting* (London: Allen and Unwin, 1974).

Callow, Simon, *Acting in Restoration Comedy* (New York: Applause, 1991).

Downes, Kerry, *Sir John Vanbrugh: A Biography* (London: Sedgewick and Jackson, 1987).

Downes, Kerry, *The Prison, the Castle and the Palace. Sir John Vanbrugh: A Biography* (London: Peter Holland, 1988).

Harris, Bernard, *Sir John Vanbrugh* (London: Longman, 1967).

Husboe, Arthur R., *Sir John Vanbrugh* (Boston: Twayne, 1986).

McCormick, Frank, *Sir John Vanbrugh: The Playwright as Architect* (Pennsylvania: Pennsylvania State University Press, 1991).

McCormick, Frank, *Sir John Vanbrugh: A Reference Guide* (New York: Hall, 1992).

Whistler, Lawrence, *Sir John Vanbrugh, Architect and Dramatist 1664–1726* (New York: Millwood, 1978).

Articles

Barlow, Graham F., 'Vanbrugh's Queens Theatre in the Haymarket', *Early Music*, vol. 17 (November 1989), pp. 515–21.

Berkowitz, Gerald M., 'Sir John Vanbrugh and the Conventions of Restoration Comedy', *Genre*, vol. 6 (1973), pp. 346–61.

Brooks, Harold F., 'Principle Conflicts in the Restoration Comedy of Manners: The Battle of Sex and Truewits v. Witwouds and Lackwits', *Durham University Journal*, vol. 49 (1988), pp. 201–12.

Chiapelli, Carolyn, 'The Single Plot Structure of Vanbrugh's *The Relapse*', *English Miscellany*, vols 28–9 (1980), pp. 207–25.

Coleman, Antony, 'Sir John Brute on the Eighteenth Century Stage',

Restoration and Eighteenth Century Theatre Research, vol. 8 (ii) (1969), pp. 41–6.

Cordner, Michael, 'Time, the Churches, and Vanbrugh's Lord Foppington', *Durham University Journal*, vol. 77 (1984–5), pp. 11–17.

Faller, Lincoln, 'Betwixt Jest and Earnest: The Comedy of Sir John Vanbrugh', *Modern Philology*, vol. 72 (1974–5), pp. 17–29.

Finke, Laurie, 'Virtue in Fashion: The Fate of Women in Comedies of Cibber and Vanbrugh', in Robert Markley and Laurie Finke, *From Renaissance to Restoration: Metamorphosis of the Drama* (Cleveland: Bellflower Press, 1984), pp. 155–79.

Gill, J. E., 'Character, Plot and the Landscape of Love in *The Relapse*: A Re-appraisal', *Studies in English Literary Culture*, vol. 16 (ii) (1992), pp. 110–25.

Hughes, Derek, 'Cibber and Vanbrugh: Language, Place and Social Order in *Love's Last Shift*', *Comparative Drama*, vol. 20 (iv) (1986), pp. 287–304.

Hughes, Derek, 'Vanbrugh and Cibber: Language, Place and Social Order in *The Relapse*', *Comparative Drama*, vol. 21 (1988), pp. 62–83.

Mueschke, Paul and Jeanette Fleisher, 'A Re-evaluation of Vanbrugh', *Publications of the Modern Language Association*, vol. 49 (1934), pp. 848–89.

Olleson, Philip, 'Vanbrugh and the Opera at the Queens Theatre, Haymarket', *Theatre Notebook*, vol. 26 (1972), pp. 94–101.

Olshen, Barry N., 'The Original and Improved Comedies of Sir John Vanbrugh: Their Nineteenth Century London Stage History', *Restoration and Eighteenth Century Theatre Research*, vol. 13 (i) (1974), pp. 27–52.

General Bibliography

Books

Alleman, G. S., *Matrimonial Law and Restoration Comedy* (Philadelphia, 1942).

Bahlman, Dudley, *The Moral Revolution of 1688* (New Haven: Yale University Press, 1957).

Bevis, Richard, *English Drama: 1660–1789* (London: Longman, 1988).

Boswell, Eleanore, *The Restoration Court Stage 1660–1702* (London: Allen and Unwin, 1932).

Burns, Edward, *Restoration Comedy: Crises of Desire and Identity* (London: Macmillan, 1987).

Cibber, Colley, *An Apology for the Life of Colley Cibber, Written by Himself* (ed. R. W. Lowe) (London, 1889).

Cibber, Colley, *Dramatic Works*, 5 volumes (New York: Ams Press, 1966).

Collier, Jeremy, *A Short View of the Immorality and Prophaneness of the English Stage* (1698), in Scott McMillin (ed.), *Restoration and Eighteenth Century Comedy* (London: Norton, 1973), pp. 494–504.

Collier, Jeremy, *A Defence of the Short View of the Immorality and Prophaneness of the English Stage* (London, 1699).

Cope, Jackson, *Dramaturgy of the Daemonic: Studies in Antigeneric Theatre from Ruzante to Grimaldi* (Baltimore: Johns Hopkins University Press, 1984).

Craik, T. W. (ed.), *Revels History of Drama in English, 1660–1750* (London: Methuen, 1976).

Dobree, Bonamy, *Restoration Comedy 1660–1720* (London: Oxford University Press, 1924).

Eddershaw, Margaret, *Performing Brecht: Forty Years of British Performances* (London: Routledge, 1996).

Gaskill, William, *A Sense of Direction* (London: Faber and Faber, 1988).

Genest, J., *Some Account of the English Stage, from the Restoration to 1830*, 10 volumes (Bath, 1832).

Gill, Pat, *Interpreting Ladies: Women, Wit and Morality in the Restoration Comedy of Manners* (London: University of Georgia, 1994).

Harbage, Arthur, *Cavalier Drama: An Historical and Critical Supplement to the Study of the Elizabethan and Restoration Stage* (New York: Modern Language Association, 1936).

Hellinger, Bernard, *A Short View of the Immorality and Prophaneness of the English Stage: A Critical Edition* (New York: Garland, 1987).

Hill, Christopher, *The Century of Revolution* (London: Sphere, 1969).

Holland, Norman M., *The First Modern Comedies: The Significance of Etherege, Wycherley and Congreve* (Cambridge, MA: Harvard University Press, 1959).

Holland, Pat, *The Ornament of Action: Text and Performance in Restoration Comedy* (Cambridge: Cambridge University Press, 1979).

Holmes, Geoffrey, *The Making of a Great Power: Late Stuart and Early Georgian Britain 1660–1722* (London: Longman, 1993).

Hulmes, R. D. (ed.), *The London Theatre World, 1660–1800* (New Haven: Yale University Press, 1980).

Hume, Robert, *The Development of English Drama in the Late Seventeenth Century* (Oxford: Clarendon, 1976).

Krutch, Joseph Wood, *Comedy and Conscience after the Restoration* (New York: Columbia University Press, 1924).

Leacroft, Richard, *The Development of the English Playhouse* (London: Eyre Methuen, 1973).

Loftis, John, *Comedy and Society from Congreve to Fielding*, Stanford Studies in Language and Literature, 19 (Stanford: Stanford University Press, 1959).

Loftis, John, *The Politics of Drama in Augustan England* (Oxford: Oxford University Press, 1963).

Loftis, John (ed.), *Restoration Drama: Modern Essays in Criticism* (Oxford: Oxford University Press, 1966).

Lynch, Kathleen, *The Social Mode of Restoration Comedy* (New York: University of Michigan Press, 1926).

Mignon, Elizabeth, *Crabbed Age and Youth* (Durham, NC: Duke University Press, 1947).

Milhous, Judith, *Thomas Betteron and the Management of Lincoln's Inn Field* (Carbondale: University of Southern Illinois Press, 1979).

Milhous, Judith and Robert Hume, *Producible Interpretation: Eight English Plays 1675–1707* (Carbondale: University of Southern Illinois Press, 1985).

Palmer, John, *The Comedy of Manners* (London: Bell, 1913).

Pearson, Jacqueline, *The Prostituted Muse: Images of Women and Women Dramatists 1642–1737* (New York: St Martin's Press, 1988).

Plumb, J. H., *The Growth of Political Stability in England 1675–1725* (Harmondsworth: Penguin, 1969).

Powell, Jocelyn, *Restoration Theatre Production* (London: Routledge, 1984).

Roberts, David, *The Ladies: Female Patronage of Restoration Drama 1660–1700* (Oxford: Oxford University Press, 1989).

Sinden, Donald, *Laughter in the Second Act* (London: Hodder and Stoughton, 1985).

Singh, Sarup, *The Theory of Drama in the Restoration Period* (Calcutta: Orient Longmans, 1963).

Smith, John Harrington, *The Gay Couple in Restoration Comedy* (Cambridge, MA: Harvard University Press, 1948).

Southern, Richard, *Changeable Scenery* (London: Faber and Faber, 1952).

Staves, Susan, *Players' Scepters: Fictions of Authority in the Restoration* (London: University of Nebraska Press, 1979).

Steele, Sir Richard, Preface, in Shirley Strum Kenny (ed.), *The Conscious Lovers* (London: Arnold, 1968).

Styan, J. L., *Restoration Comedy in Performance* (Cambridge: Cambridge University Press, 1986).

Summers, Montague, *Restoration Theatre* (London: Kegan Paul, 1934).

Thomas, David (ed.), *Restoration and Georgian England 1660–1788*, in the series Theatre in Europe: A Documentary History (Cambridge: Cambridge University Press, 1989).

Tracts on the British Stage 1699–1726 (British Library: 641. e. 16).

Underwood, Dale, *Etherege and the Seventeenth Century Comedy of Manners* (New Haven: Yale University Press, 1957).

Wain, John, 'Restoration Comedy and its Modern Critics', *Preliminary Essays* (London: Macmillan, 1957).

Wells, S. B. (ed.), *Charles Gildon's* A Comparison Between the Two Stages (Princeton: Princeton University Press, 1942).

Wilcox, John, *The Relation of Molière to Restoration Comedy* (New York: Columbia University Press, 1938).

Zimbardo, Rose A., *A Mirror to Nature: Transformations in Drama and Aesthetics 1660–1732* (Lexington, KY: University Press of Kentucky, 1986).

Articles

Birca, Sancha de, 'Floosies and Their Fops', *Plays and Players* (June 1985), pp. 10–11.

Cranfield, Douglas, 'Religious Language and Religious Meaning in Restoration Comedy', *Studies in English Literature*, vol. 20 (1980), pp. 385–406.

Cordner, Michael, 'Marriage Comedy After the 1688 Revolution: Southerne to Vanbrugh', *Modern Language Review*, vol. 85 (ii) (1990), pp. 273–89.

Habakkuk, J., 'Marriage settlements in the Eighteenth Century', *Transactions of the Royal History Society*, 4th series, vol. 32 (1950).

Hume, Robert, 'Marital Discord in English Comedy from Dryden to Fielding', *Modern Philology*, vol. 74 (1976–7), pp. 248–72.

Kenny, Shirley Strum, 'Perennial Favourites: Congreve, Wycherley, Vanbrugh, Cibber, Farquhar and Steele', *Modern Philology*, vol. 73/4 (ii) (1976), pp. 4–11.

Kenny, Shirley Strum, 'Humane Comedy', *Modern Philology*, vol. 75 (1977), pp. 29–43.

Kenny, Shirley Strum, 'Elopements, Divorce and the Devil Knows What: Love and Marriage in British Comedy, 1690–1720', *South Atlantic Quarterly*, vol. 78 (1979), pp. 84–106.

Langhans, Edward, 'Wren's Restoration Playhouse', *Theatre Notebook*, vol. 18 (1964).

Langhans, Edward, 'A Conjectural Reconstruction of the Dorset Garden Theatre', *Theatre Survey*, vol. 13 (1972).

Langhans, Edward, 'New Early Eighteenth Century Performances and Casts', *Theatre Notebook*, vol. 26 (iv) (1972), pp. 145–6.

Langhans, Edward, 'Players and Playhouses, 1695–1710 and Their Effects on English Comedy', *Theatre Annual*, vol. 29 (1973), pp. 28–39.

Love, Harold, 'Who were the Restoration Audience?', *Yearbook of English Studies, Volume X. Literature and its Audience* (eds G. K. Hunter and C. J. Rawson) (London: Modern Humanities Research Association, 1980), pp. 21–44.

Martin, Lee, 'From Forestage to Proscenium: A Study of Restoration Staging Techniques', *Theatre Survey*, vol. 4 (1963), pp. 3–28.

McDonald, Charles, 'Restoration Comedy as Drama of Satire: An Investigation Into Seventeenth Century Aesthetics', *Studies in Philology*, vol. 61 (iii) (1964), pp. 522–44.

Neill, Michael, 'Heroic Heads and Humble Tails: Sex, Politics and the Restoration Comic Race', *The Eighteenth Century: Theory and Interpretation*, vol. 24 (ii) (1983), pp. 115–39.

Parnell, Paul, 'Equivocation in Cibber's Love's Last Shift', *SP*, vol. 57 (1960), pp. 519–34.

Rodway, Alan, 'Restoration Comedy Re-examined', *Renaissance and Modern Studies*, vol. 16 (1972), pp. 37–60.

Scouten, Arthur and Robert Hume, 'Restoration Comedy and its Audiences, 1660–1776', *Yearbook of English Studies, Volume X. Literature and its Audience* (eds G. K. Hunter and C. J. Rawson) (London: Modern Humanities Research Association, 1980), pp. 45–69.

Index